INFORMATION PROCESSING FOR BUS

INFORMATION PROCESSING FOR BUSINESS STUDIES

A. E. Innes
BSc(Econ)(Hons), DPA(Lond), Cert Ed(Leeds)

PITMAN PUBLISHING
128 Long Acre, London WC2E 9AN

© Alex Innes 1987

First published in Great Britain 1987

British Library Cataloguing in Publication Data

Innes, Alex
 Information processing for business studies.
 1. Business—Data processing
 I. Title
 658'.05   HF5548.2
ISBN 0-273-02540-6

All rights reserved. No part of this publication may be reproduced, stored in a retrieval system, or transmitted, in any form or by any means, electronic, mechanical, photocopying, recording and/or otherwise, without the prior written permission of the publishers. This book may not be lent, resold, hired out or otherwise disposed of by way of trade in any form of binding or cover other than that in which it is published, without the prior consent of the publishers.

Printed in Great Britain at The Bath Press, Avon.

CONTENTS

Preface vi
Acknowledgments viii
1 Data, information and management 1
2 Introducing systems 15
3 Information systems 28
4 The electronic computer and its place in business 36
5 The storage of data 48
6 Input and output methods 58
7 Processing routines 76
8 Main-frame and other computers 93
9 Computer services 99
10 Software 105
11 Staff and departments 112
12 The electronic office and its setting 120
13 Data transmission techniques and services 132
14 Introducing computer systems to organisations 142
15 Charts, diagrams and software for simple projects 152
16 Problems of security, privacy and social change 175
Bibliography 186
Index 189

Publisher's note

For ease of grammatical expression and presentation the author has resorted to masculine third person, singular pronouns and adjectives in this text. He intends no discourtesy to female readers, who are asked to substitute appropriate female pronouns and adjectives where required.

PREFACE

The main purpose of this book is to provide a through text for students taking BTEC National Awards examinations in Information Processing 1 (J185) and Information Processing 2 (J186). Given adequate resources and the carrying out of practical work, as required by the Option Modules, these students' reading requirements should be well met, and teachers' problems in devising practical assignments considerably eased. Chapters 1–13 cover J185, and the addition of Chapters 14–16 covers J186.

The book could also serve as a primary text for data and information processing at elementary level, and as background or introductory reading for examinations in these subjects at higher level; the inclusion of 'other examination questions' at the end of each chapter illustrates the point.

Businessmen, administrators and others requiring a readable, cohesive and comprehensive account of modern information processing should find the book useful.

The changing of the Option Modules from Data Processing to Information Processing raised the possibility that mere revision of the author's 2nd edition of *Data Processing for Business Studies*, published in 1984, would not meet the new needs. There were good reasons for this: the new modules contained a significant amount of new material, and demanded a more practical approach; in two years of rapidly developing technology, information processing had changed and expanded noticeably; and in a new book it would be easier to strengthen treatment of some topics on lines suggested by private reviews which the first publishers had received of the data-processing book.

Studying a modern subject like information processing brings for the newcomer certain learning difficulties. A large number of new technical devices and processes must be studied, as seen for example in Chapter 6 on the input and output of data. A new, un-English vocabulary must be mastered, with a given word sometimes taking a shade of meaning reflecting an expert's preference and depending on whether the dialect is British or American. The whole subject could soon become a miscellaneous collection of fairly small, separate packets of information, with examination success obtainable by pure memorisation, and the objects of study being thankfully discarded as soon as the ordeal has ended. To meet the problem, technical details have been set in realistic examples, individual descriptions have been built into accounts of larger systems, and emphasis has been put on reasons and purposes served rather than on minutiae. The author's hope is that students will gain an understanding of information processing, a facility in application and a curiosity which will lead to further study.

Exercises of four kinds follow each chapter. The 'short questions' are like those which have been favourably received by users of the data-processing book: they are intended to consolidate and develop the text and, in some cases, to prepare the ground for what follows; they do not require a pointless location and re-hashing of bits of the text. 'Practical exercises' are on the lines of BTEC assignments. To all students, they should help to consolidate and amplify the topics in the chapter. In writing them, the author has drawn on both practical and examining experience. The approach may, for some readers, appear novel, but the methods work. 'Questions relevant to BTEC written examinations' are of a level and type which could reasonably be expected in formal papers for these examinations. These three types of exercise mainly relate to the subject-matter of the chapter they follow, and do not require knowledge of later chapters, except in a few cases where practical exercises direct the reader to particular parts of the later text. 'Other examination questions' relate mainly to the subject of the parent chapter, but may require reference to other chapters.

A. E. Innes
Canterbury 1986

ACKNOWLEDGMENTS

Once again, I gladly acknowledge help from a number of sources.

The editorial staff of Macdonald and Evans Ltd, where the outlines of the book were developed, and of Pitman Publishing Ltd, where it took final shape, have been both encouraging and helpful.

Mr Alan Powell, joint managing director of Pelltech Ltd, Witney, a firm distributing drawing office equipment and stationery, gave valuable insight into the recent introduction and operation of a small computer system. Through Mr Peter Brown, manager, I was able to obtain valuable information about the characteristics of local authority information-processing systems, at the centre jointly run by Thanet and Dover District Councils. Pitman Publishing Ltd Computing Centre gave information about a publisher's system, supported with a wealth of illustrative print-outs.

Mercury Communications Ltd, the local office of British Telecom, and the local and regional offices of the Post Office were most generous in supplying written information on data transmission and other systems, and it would require a much larger book to do justice to all of it.

I am grateful to the following examining bodies for permission to quote from past examination papers, and I give the abbreviations under which they are identified in the chapters:

Association of Accounting Technicians (AAT);
Chartered Association of Certified Accountants (ACCA);
City and Guilds of London Institute (CGLI);
Chartered Institute of Public Finance and Accountancy (CIPFA);
Institute of Administrative Management (IAM);
Institute of Cost and Management Accountants (ICMA);
Institute of Data Processing Management (IDPM);
Institute of Management Services (IMS);
Royal Society of Arts (RSA).

Two friends have been most helpful. Mr Martin Neeve, BEd, who is teacher in mathematics and in charge of computer studies at Sir Roger Manwood Grammar School, Sandwich, Kent, read all the chapters, and advised on the practical work. Mr Michael May, BSc, head of mathematics and business studies at Conyngham School, Ramsgate, Kent, gave much help on the programs and text in Chapter 15.

I am again greatly indebted to my typist, Mrs Beryl Perry. At times, the speed of input of manuscript must have put her under strain: but the output of typescript was so prompt and of such a high standard that there was no evidence of it.

I have tried to keep my account relevant, accurate and up-to-date, and I take full responsibility if at any point I have failed to do so.

A. E. Innes
Canterbury, 1986

1 DATA, INFORMATION AND MANAGEMENT

> This chapter
> - introduces the terms *data* and *information*;
> - explains how they differ;
> - discusses their importance in businesses and organisations;
> - illustrates how processing them helps in decision making.

Facts in business and organisation

The subject of this book, *information processing*, is an operation extensively carried out in businesses and other organisations today. The operations are concerned with *facts*, defined simply as true statements. Selections of such facts are used by management in making important decisions. Figure 1.1 outlines a typical manufacturing business to illustrate facts from which a selection could be made.

The meanings of the terms *input* and *output* are self-evident here for they refer to raw materials and finished goods respectively. Later in the book they will be used extensively to describe a variety of things, for example documents which enter a given process, such as invoices, and those that emerge, such as quarterly statements of account.

The following are examples of six facts, two for each stage, relating to the business.

Input
1 All timber used is imported from Scandinavia.
2 The cost of paint to the firm increased by 12 per cent over 1984.

Factory
1 The factory is situated on the Enterprise Trading Estate, Northcaster.
2 The factory building is insured against fire in the sum of £300,000 with the Settlefast Fire Corporation.

Output
1 35 per cent of items sold were to DIY businesses.

2 25 coffee tables, type ET/2, were delivered to Northcaster Home Supplies Ltd on 22 October 1984.

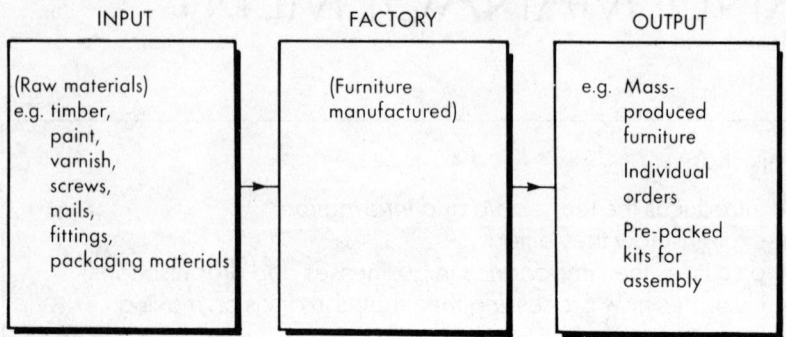

Fig. 1.1 Physical input and output of a furniture factory

Data

Literally, *data* means 'things given'. The singular is *datum*. In business practice, the word data is increasingly used to refer to one or more, and takes a singular verb, whatever the number of items. In the context of information processing, data means a fact or facts prepared for entry into an electronic computer, generally as a matter of routine.

Item 2 under Output above is an example. This group of facts would be put into the manufacturer's computer to enable an invoice and a statement of account to be prepared. Another example would be the following information found on the detachable slip of a DHSS pension or allowance order book (see Figs 1.2*a* and 1.2*b*):

Pension/allowance no.   (A);
Serial no.   (B);
Not exceeding (pounds)   (C);
Due on and not before   (D).

The data consists of:

(A) (figures and letters);
(B) (figures);
(C) (amount to be paid);
(D) (date of payment).

A further fact (E) is the date of payment as imprinted at the office where payment is made.

When a pension or allowance is paid, the slip is stamped, detached and sent on to the DHSS computer for recording. (See Fig. 1.2*c*.)

Data, information and management **3**

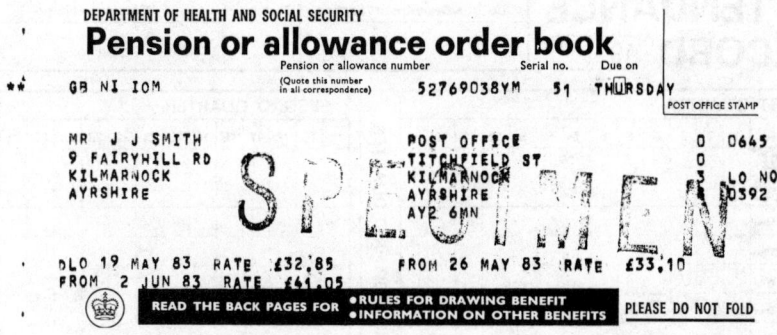

Fig. 1.2a   Front page of a pension or allowance order book (*Crown Copyright*)

Fig. 1.2b   'Tear off' page of a pension or allowance order book (*Crown Copyright*)

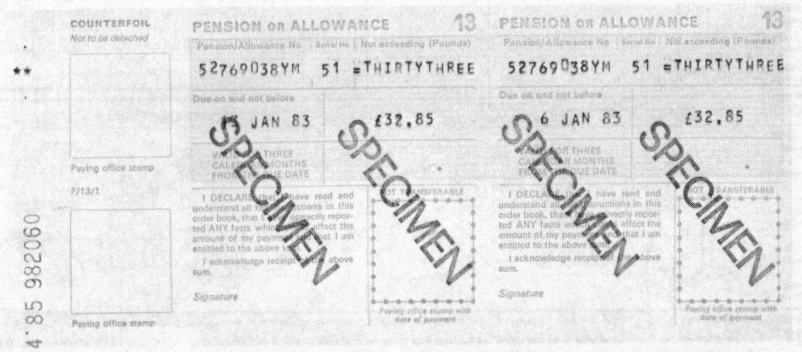

Fig. 1.2c   Slip detached from book by post office upon payment and forwarded for processing (*Crown Copyright*)

4 Information Processing for Business Studies

Fig. 1.3 Attendance Record Form (reproduced by permission of IPM Personnel Management Ltd and Formecon Services Ltd)

Data processing

Facts entering a computer as data pass through stages, which will be described in detail in later chapters. The working of a computerised pay-roll involves a large number of stages. Central to the operation will be the calculation of the gross pay of each worker. Items of data required for this will include:

- Name of each worker;
- Each worker's number;
- Classification of each worker (e.g. manual, part-time, etc.);
- Number of hours in standard week;
- Hours worked in that week by the worker;
- Normal hourly rates;
- Overtime rates.

Figures 1.3 and 1.4 show documents used in two different systems.

The details will be fed from documents such as time-sheets and union booklets stating agreed hourly rates. Calculations of gross pay will be made by analysing each worker's hours for the week into standard hours and overtime, applying two different rates and adding the sub-totals.

Data can be entered into the computer in various ways. In pay-roll operations the computer will probably take the data from electronically recorded devices called *files*, which serve the same kind of functions as ordinary office files. Two files which could be used are:

1 Nominal file – gives the name and works number of each worker.
2 Hourly rate file – gives standard and overtime rates for a variety of workers.

Data processing is the term which describes the stages through which items of data pass until they leave the complete computing process. In this example, a number of different kinds of operations occur, for example:

1 Clerk reads figures written by worker on his time sheet, and puts them on a file by an electronic device.
2 Data is transferred from File A to File B.
3 In the computer, a standard rate of pay is multiplied by a number of hours.
4 In the computer one worker's gross pay is temporarily stored until that of every other worker is calculated.
5 The computer prints out in readable form the week's pay-roll.

Each of the stages listed, or the complete operation, is an example of *data processing*. Data processing consists of any operation by which data changes its location or form, or both.

6 Information Processing for Business Studies

COMPANY UK Stores Ltd		EMPLOYEE Lam, Kim Ms.			
		CUMULATIVE TO DATE			
DATE 23.8. ...	GROSS 1834	GROSS TAXABLE 1834	TAX 306.50	N I CONTRIBUTIONS 164.85	
	TAX CODE	PREVIOUS EMPLOYMENT			
PERIOD TAX 21	BASIC CODE 200L	GROSS	TAX	ANALYSIS CODE 613	EMP 5
GROSS PAY Basic 87.00		DEDUCTIONS Tax 16.40 Nat. Ins. 7.85		HOURS 35 p.w.	OVERTIME 2 hrs
				RATE 2.41	ADDITIONAL 7.26
				HOLIDAY CREDITS -	
				EMPLOYERS CONTRIBUTIONS N.I. Current 9.12 N.I. Cum. 191.52	
BROUGHT FORWARD				Payments Cheque	Carried Forward
TOTAL PAY 94.26		TOTAL DEDUCTIONS 24.25		NET PAY 70.01	

Fig. 1.4 Pay slip

Further use of routine data

When computers were first introduced to business, the main reason was to speed up standard clerical operations and reduce their costs. Pay-roll operations like those just described were a popular example. Stock control and invoicing were other common examples. But these routines generated a large amount of data, some of which could be of further use to management. Analysis of pay data over a period of time could show what overtime was being worked, its trend and whether absences through sickness were below or above average at a given time of the year. Once the computer was installed, the extra details could be quickly obtained at relatively low cost.

Furthermore, although the operation of a computer is based upon very simple processes, given suitable instructions it can be made to perform calculations of extraordinary magnitude and complexity. A transport firm, for example, working with a variety of vehicles, loads and routes, can through a computer plan its use of vehicles and journeys to minimise its costs. The prosperity of an insurance company will very much depend upon the way in which it invests its fluctuating premium funds. Given adequate, up-to-date incoming data, its computer can show how this can be best done to meet criteria of profitability, liquidity and security. If a firm's invoices are well

Data, information and management 7

```
┌─────────────────────────────────────────────────────────────────┐
│  Invoice No:   6713/D      ELECTRO SUPPLIES                     │
│  Order No:     577B        (Hong Kong) Ltd.                     │
│  Date:     9 June 19 ..    352 Westlands Road                   │
│                            Quarry Bay                           │
│                            Hong Kong                            │
│                                                                 │
│   International Importers Inc.                                  │
│   605 West 50th Street                                          │
│   New York 10020                                                │
│   USA                                                           │
│                                                                 │
│  Tel: 6-884115-3       Telex: 5528 EK     Cable: LECTRON        │
│                                                                 │
│   Cat. No.          Items                    Price $US          │
│                                                                 │
│   C451/N      500 VHS Video Tapes  @ $2.00 each    1000.00      │
│   C511/N      1000 cassette     "  @ $1.20   "     1200.00      │
│   E 61/0      5 VDUs (Standard)    @ $300.00"      1500.00      │
│   D 51/E      30 cass. records.    @ $40.00  "     1200.00      │
│                                                                 │
│                                                    4900.00      │
│                                 Add 10% tax         490.00      │
│                                                                 │
│                                                    5390.00      │
│                            Less 20% Quantity Disc. 1078.00      │
│                                                                 │
│                                                    4312.00      │
│   Add Dock Charges    50.00                                     │
│       Insurance to                                              │
│       New York        70.00                                     │
│       Freight        165.00                         285.00      │
│                                                                 │
│                                    cif New York    4597.00      │
│                                                                 │
│   E & O E                                                       │
└─────────────────────────────────────────────────────────────────┘
```

Fig. 1.5 Commercial invoice

designed, a computer can analyse their data to show geographical, social and financial aspects of the market for its product: and if the firm wishes to forecast its sales, a computer can make projections continuously adjusted to take into account the latest sales figures available.

Management functions

As this new potential of computers is developing, management is becoming more professional in its skills and status. Although the functions of different managers vary, the functions of corporate management are usually understood to include the following:

Planning

The management sets important objectives for the undertaking, and lays down the main lines by which they will be achieved.

If our furniture firm decided to increase its output by 25 per cent over three years the works manager would need to know what new machinery was to be purchased. The personnel department would work to a staff expansion programme, increases for each of the three years being specified. The finance department would lay down detailed estimates for the increased costs, set against increased returns, and changes in other parts of the firm would have to be foreseen and timetabled.

A county council providing roads for a new town must plan the purchase of land, engage civil engineering contractors and ensure that rates and government grants are available to pay for these.

Controlling

This is the function of management that ensures that what is planned is achieved.

With the factory expansion, budgets must be observed and production schedules maintained.

The county council will have to check that land purchase, site preparation and contract work do not fall behind. The function entails taking remedial action where shortcomings occur.

Co-ordination

Most management undertakings will involve subordinate parts of the organisation. The co-ordinating function brings them together, so that they work as one.

In expanding furniture output the works manager must work with the personnel department to ensure that the right number of extra workers with the appropriate skills are engaged. The purchasing department must co-operate with the production department if an uninterrupted flow of raw materials is to be available.

The problem of co-ordination in building new roads is even greater than in a manufacturing enterprise, because a county council performs a number of functions in a democratic system run by part-time lay representatives. Co-ordination means, for example, that the legal committee and its staff negotiate land purchases in good time, and that highway developments are consistent with land-use policy. Close co-operation must be sought between the council's highway engineers and public authorities whose utilities such as water mains, sewerage pipes or electricity cables are likely to lie under road surfaces.

Motivating

Ultimately, the success of any project depends upon securing the full co-operation of all the people who will have to carry it out.

To expand furniture production, the managing director will need to convince the management team that this objective, and the plans for achieving it, are in the firm's best interests. Workers will only give of their best if they are assured that the proposals for increased output will not presently lead to over-stocking and unemployment.

The function of management which evokes the best response from human resources is known as motivating. Generally, it is more difficult to exercise in publicly owned enterprises than in those privately owned, but some scope for *leadership*, to use an alternative term, is offered. Incentive bonuses can be paid to highway construction workers. Good relationships between the council and the press will prove an incentive to professional and technical staff for whom ordinary incentive schemes would be unsuitable.

Decision making

The business of public undertakings will succeed if the policy decisions its management makes are sound. Two important factors will determine the soundness of these decisions:

1 the adequacy and relevance of the facts used in making the decision;
2 the judgment of management in shaping policy from those factors.

Factor 2 lies outside the scope of this book. The special kind of facts used in 1 are the subject of this book and are explained in the next paragraph.

Information

Data which conveys a message to someone is called 'information', so that *management information* is meaningful to management.

A computer used by a furniture manufacturing firm could undertake the routine clerical work of purchasing. A record could be kept of suppliers of raw material, with provision for deleting those no longer used and adding new ones. Suppliers' accounts could be checked and, where agreed, the computer could print out cheques and adjust the accounts thus settled. Once the scheme was agreed by management, it would normally work without further reference to management. Data relating to sales, deliveries, return of faulty materials, etc., would be processed almost automatically. An efficient management would continuously seek to improve the firm's performance by reducing costs, increasing returns and improving the quality of its products. On the input side it would review from time to time the performances of suppliers where competition existed for the furniture firm's business. Documents and files used in the routine clerical operations would yield data on such criteria as:

- delivery times;
- discounts allowed by suppliers;
- reliability of supply service;
- quality of materials;
- transport charges, etc.

Experience would suggest the relative importance of such factors when judging suppliers. Management could call at set intervals, such as quarterly or annually, for special reports on suppliers to guide its purchasing policy. Such reports are examples of *management reports*.

Public bodies as well as private enterprises make use of management information. In local government a district council will manage existing housing estates and through contract or a direct labour department put up new houses. Examples of computerised data are:

- roll of tenants;
- rents received;
- records of repairs and maintenance;
- bills of quantities (statements of quantities of materials and costs, e.g. of metre run of 3 cm copper pipe, prepared by surveyors and included in building contracts).

The 'management', i.e. the housing manager acting under the housing committee, will be very little concerned with such data. If a change in policy is proposed, e.g. to improve the amenities of pre-war houses on a large scale, or to appoint new officials to guard against vandals, some of this data and probably other data, e.g. from the council's establishment department, will be needed. Calculations such as forecasts of rising material costs will need to be made, and the financial consequences of alternative policies will need to be assessed. The organised facts produced by the computer will be management information.

Facts, data and information

The relationship between these three terms can be shown in a simple diagram (Fig. 1.6).

Data, information and management

1   Includes all the true statements that can be made about a business or organisation.
2   Data-facts that are entered directly into the computer or stored in a form suitable for later entry.
3   Facts not needed for 4 or 5.
4   Data formed into reports for management.
5   Data used by the firm or organisation for purposes other than management information.

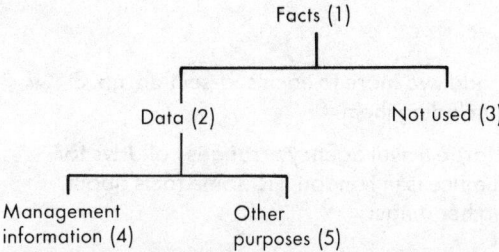

Fig. 1.6 Analysis of business facts

Particular items of data under 2 may enter into both 4 and 5. For example, the weekly mileage of a particular vehicle run by a road transport firm may be included in the records printed out each week to monitor servicing: at the same time, it may be passed on to the police to help enquiries about alleged falsification of a tachograph record.

Management information in practice

If computing facilities are to be exploited to their full, then a scheme will be designed to relate the gathering of data and management information to all parts of the firm or organisation. The next chapter describes the basis of such schemes.

Terms and definitions

The computer age has created a new technical language. Of necessity many of its terms are simply adaptation of older words to computing situations, or new words made from precomputing word roots. Most of the terms used in this book are defined in *A Glossary of Computing Terms for Introductory Courses* produced by the British Computer Society. Where the glossary is on the reading list of a course or examination, important definitions will clearly need to be learnt. However, definitions given in computing and related books of the same terms often vary in detail and sometimes in emphasis. BTEC National Specification for Information Processing 1 (J185) requires a distinction to be made between data and information, whereas some books make the terms almost synonymous. Readers of this chapter will notice that important terms have been explained in their working contexts, and rigid definitions have not been given; this practice will be followed in the rest of the book. Once a term has been introduced its established connotation will be consistently maintained.

Short questions

1 To the facts listed on p. 11, add two more to each sub-section, no. 3 including quantities, no. 4 not including them.

2 A Manchester branch of a large travel agency arranges holidays for customers who visit it. Its head office is in London. List some facts about its business under the following headings:

Customers' enquiries at the branch;
Communications between the branch and head office;
The arranging of holidays by the firm.

3 Use a business example different from those given in the text to explain the difference between facts and data, giving two illustrations.

4 Records of a state hospital's resident- and out-patients are computerised.

   (a) Excluding patients' names, ages, sexes and addresses, give *six* examples of items of data likely to be recorded.
   (b) Assume that much more data than this is kept relating to each patient. Data is also kept under a number of other headings, e.g. medical staff, nursing staff, supplies, etc.
      (i) Give two more headings covered by 'etc.'.
      (ii) Explain how some of this data could help
         I – a surgical specialist;
         II – the hospital's board of management.

5 Show that you understand the difference between the terms 'data' and 'information' by giving examples of each for the following:

   (a) an oil firm prospecting in the North Sea;
   (b) a public library;
   (c) a charitable body providing homes for the aged.

Assume in each case that the organisation is being run with the help of a computer.

6 Choosing *either* a commercial bank *or* an insurance company, and using the four management functions given in the chapter, give an example of a management decision that would fit that function.

7 Describe the data and information which would be useful to the management in making *one* of the decisions given in your answer to question 6.

Practical work

1 Take a recent example of a national newspaper of interest to the general reader. Study news items, comments and advertisements.

  (*a*) List any direct references to computers.
  (*b*) Give, where possible:

   (*i*) three examples of business facts;
   (*ii*) three examples of tables of figures quoted;
   (*iii*) two examples of management-type decisions, one by a business firm, one by a public authority.

  (*c*) As you peruse the newspaper, make a written note of any other points relating to Chapter 1.

2 An organisation chart is a diagram showing how the parts of a firm or other organisation, e.g. the board of directors, the finance department and a sub-department, the cashiers' office, are related to one another. Find a fairly simple example from text books you use, from books in the business, management or administration section of a library, or directly from a local business. On the chart, the lines linking the departments represent the flow of communications and documents in one and sometimes in two directions.

  (*a*) Identify each line with a capital letter.
  (*b*) Give examples of documents and oral communications you would expect to travel along the lines, stating the direction taken.
  (*c*) Give examples of:

   (*i*) data travelling the linking lines;
   (*ii*) information that could reach management.

Questions relevant to BTEC written examinations

1 (*a*) Describe the difference between *data processing* and *information processing*.
  (*b*) Give three examples of items of data, each of which could occur in routine processing and also be used to supply management information, explaining briefly how this second use would occur.

2 Management of an undertaking is concerned with the following activities:

  (*i*) planning;
  (*ii*) controlling;
  (*iii*) co-ordinating.

(a) Give an example of a decision of each type, and the way in which computerised information processing could help management in making it. One of your examples at least should be taken from the public sector.

(b) Using one of your examples, select an item of data which was available, but which would not be used for management information. What do you conclude from this?

Other examination questions

1 Discuss the use of computers in improving managerial decision making. (IMS – Information Systems I, Nov. 1985)

2 It is generally accepted that effective management is impossible without information.

You are required to

(a) define information;
(b) discuss the characteristics of information that assists the key management functions of planning, control and decision making; and
(c) describe how to assess whether it is worthwhile producing more information for use in a particular decision.

(ICMA – Management Information Systems and Data Processing, May 1984)

2 INTRODUCING SYSTEMS

> This chapter
> - introduces the term *system*;
> - applies the term to businesses and other organisations;
> - explains the related terms *boundary*, *sub-system*, *hierarchy*, *environment*;
> - describes changes within systems, and, in particular, feedbacks;
> - discusses the value of the systems approach.

The meaning of system

One example of a *system* concerned with management information is the scheme mentioned on p. 11 towards the end of Chapter 1. The term is so widely used and refers to such a variety of arrangements that the attempt to define it in the context of information processing is better delayed until some important examples of its use have been examined.

In natural science, the sun and certain astronomical bodies which are related to it are collectively called the *solar system*. The devices such as boilers, radiators, pipes, pumps, thermostats and fuel supplies used to warm buildings are called *heating systems*. The latter kind of system is man-made and has a well defined purpose. The solar and other like systems are certainly not man-made, and if we find in them a purpose, then we infer it according to our personal philosophy, and not because we know why it was installed in a house or office-building. Most scholars studying society would claim that in large communities exist groups of human beings distinguished from one another by criteria such as economic, cultural and other characteristics. They call it the *class system*. Although its reality is generally acknowledged, discussions about its causes, operation and consequences lead to acute controversy. The democratic scheme of government in the United Kingdom is called the *Cabinet system*. Like the class system, it cannot easily be defined. It undergoes historical changes, and serves democratic purposes. A proper understanding of it depends upon identifying informal working principles, known as conventions.

Finding a simple concrete definition of a system which fits all cases is not easy. But this is not to say that it is not useful in a business or organisation to label a particular arrangement as a system. The *transport system* of large manufacturing firms would include a number of things conveniently listed under simple headings.

Buildings	Garage, transport office, etc.
Equipment	Vehicles, fuel stores and pumps, maintenance tools, inspection ramps, etc.
Human resources	Transport manager, drivers, maintenance staff, etc.
Documents	Vehicle licences, petrol storage licence, drivers' time sheets, tachograph recordings.
Others	Regular routes, customers' goodwill.

These components in practice work to a common end, the collection of raw materials and the distribution of finished goods in the most efficient way. Take any one of the items away, and the performance of the whole system is impaired. The separate things which make up a system are called its *elements*, and the transport system is one example of a *business system*.

The general way in which elected members of a local Council reach their detailed decision is known as its *committee system*. Elements can be described under the general headings above. Some are listed below, with reasons for classification given in brackets.

Buildings	Committee rooms, council chamber (where committee reports are debated and voted upon).
Equipment	Typewriters, duplicators (for typing and reproducing the minutes), filing cabinets (for storing committee papers).
Human resources	Elected representatives, chairpersons (discuss and decide business), full-time departmental officers (report and advise), committee clerks (record meetings, arrange cycles of meetings, notify members and others who attend).
Documents	Notices of meetings, agendas (lists of items to be discussed), officers' reports, minutes (record of proceedings), standing orders (rules governing meeting).
Other elements	Relationship between council and committees (e.g. delegated powers, statutory requirements), powers of committees, sub-committees, working scheme (e.g. membership, frequency of meetings), relationships with press (whether advance notices, hand-outs, etc., are given to them).

Human involvement

The two brief accounts given above illustrate different ways in which human beings are involved with business and organisational systems. The more such systems become computerised, the smaller the human element and the greater the technological. For reasons to be analysed in Chapter 4, the aim is to make systems as automatic as possible. To some extent the human element in a system can be depersonalised. For example, an employed person's activities can be formally described by a job specification, and his achievements according to a formal scheme of statistical evaluation. But to understand completely how any business or other organisation works, informal patterns of human relationships must be recognised. The operation of a firm's marketing system, for example, may well be influenced by the career prospects of its deputy manager, who happens to be the managing director's son-in-law elect. Modern theories of communication and span-of-control considerations need to be taken into account in understanding how the Cabinet system works; but of equal importance are the personality of the Prime Minister, and the balance between 'wets' and 'drys' in the Cabinet, and these cannot be readily shown on the diagrams of rectangles and lines by which systems are usually represented. In discussions on systems, two-dimensional models are indispensable, but recognition of the human element is essential if theory is to be turned into sound practice.

Systems and their relationships

Figure 2.1 describes the way in which public water supply authorities work. Untreated water is gathered from such sources as upland lakes, rivers and boreholes, and conveyed to treatment centres where it is stored, treated

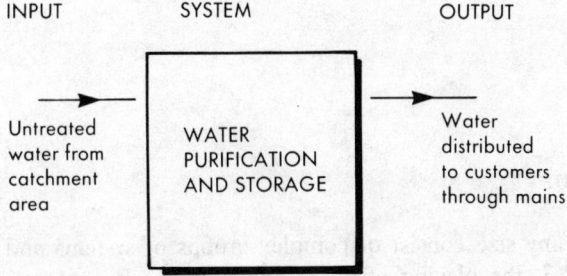

Fig. 2.1 A simple business system in its natural context

and stored again before entering the last stage of mains and control devices for final distribution to consumers. The complete process can be shown as a complex of three systems, as in Fig. 2.2.

The hard straight lines in both figures are called the *boundaries* of the system. Common boundaries between systems, shown in dotted lines, are called *interfaces*. The term also has a more specialised meaning, explained in Chapter 3.

18 Information Processing for Business Studies

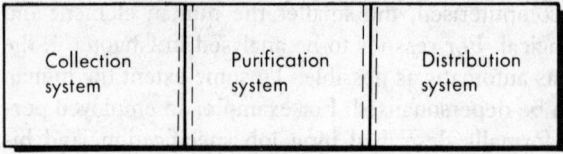

Fig. 2.2

In large organisations, *sub-systems*, i.e. sub-divisions of larger systems, are often found, as Fig. 2.3 illustrates.

Note that the term 'interface' is extended to include boundaries separating sub-systems from one another and from systems. Whether in a particular organisational structure blocks are called systems or sub-systems is a matter of convenience, and the distinction is made on the basis of the detailed working arrangements.

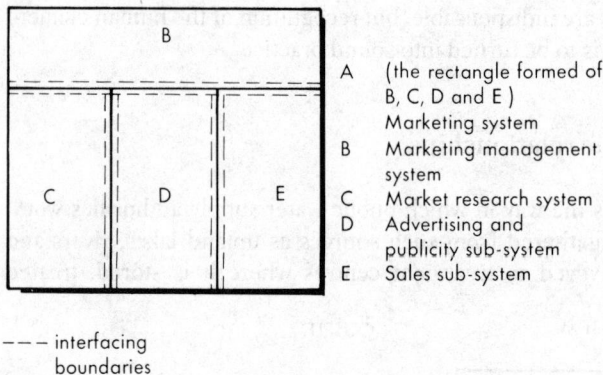

– – – interfacing boundaries

Fig. 2.3

Hierarchy of systems

Most organisations of any size consist of complex groups of systems and sub-systems. In Fig. 2.3, the placing of C, D and E under B conforms to the principle that B controls the sub-systems, and that they are answerable to it. This is a simple example of a hierarchy. Military arrangements offer the most striking example of hierarchy with a single system at the top and the broad base of a triangle at the bottom. Efficient communication between all parts of a military machine is essential for success. In the British Army in wartime at the top of the triangle would be an Army signals unit, immediately below would be several Corps signals units, and through broadening intermediate levels (e.g. Brigade) the complete structure would rest on a wide base composed of a large number of Platoon signals units.

Introducing systems **19**

Overlapping systems

Arrangements of systems and sub-systems so far have shown these as self-contained units, sharply separated from other units, although in communication with one another. Units, however, often overlap. In a domestic gas central-heating system, a supply tank, usually in the roof, will ensure that the boiler, radiators and connecting pipes are kept full of water. This part of the heating system can be looked upon as part of the water-supply system as well.

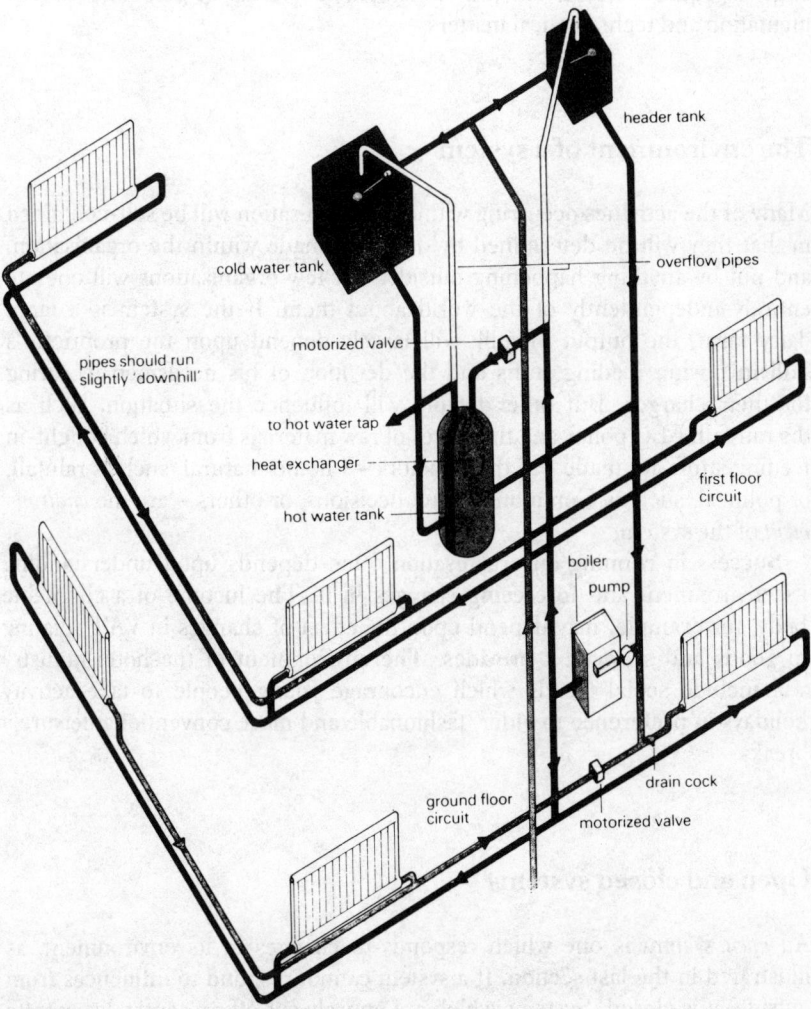

Fig. 2.4 Plan of a central heating system

In a local government committee system, a council's separate committees can be regarded as parts of sub-systems. Each department is likely to have its own committee, e.g. housing, parks and amenities, highways. The council's policy committee which is intended to co-ordinate planning and policy-making will often consist of the chairpersons of all the departmental committees. The overlapping will be intentional.

When computing was first introduced to business life, development normally occurred in the accountant's department, for applications were needed here, and it was natural to train staff with a financial and numerical background. In many organisations today, accounting and computing work as large co-equal systems, but with considerable overlap in personnel, documentation and technological matters.

The environment of a system

Many of the activities occurring within an organisation will be self-contained in that they will be determined by decisions made within the organisation, and not by anything happening outside. Yet few organisations will operate entirely independently of the world about them. If the system is a large dairy farm, the output of milk will largely depend upon the proprietor's skill in buying feeding stuffs and the devotion of his herdsmen in caring for their charges. But other factors will influence the situation, such as the rainfall, EEC policy and the prices of raw materials from which bought-in feeding stuffs are made. All these factors – whether natural, such as rainfall, or political, such as Common Market decisions, or others – are the *environment* of the system.

Success in running an organisation often depends upon understanding its environment and foreseeing changes in it. The income of a charitable body, for example, may depend upon the effect of changes in VAT relating to goods and services it provides. The environment of the hotel industry will include social trends which encourage young people to take activity holidays in preference to older, fashionable and more conventional leisurely breaks.

Open and closed systems

An *open* system is one which responds to changes in its environment, as illustrated in the last section. If a system cannot respond to influences from outside, it is closed. Systems which are entirely cut off presently degenerate and fail to achieve their purpose. Some writers define a closed system as one having no environment. In the world of human organisation it would be difficult to discover a system which was completely closed, but in designing or analysing business and other systems, especially if the time span is short rather than long, it is sometimes convenient to ignore the environment. States of increasing disorder and growing failure to fulfil functions occur from time to time in real life, but the degree of self-determination ensured by the presence of human elements in business systems usually prevents a final state of complete disorder: man-made intervention usually forestalls such a natural death.

The behaviour of systems

The word 'behaviour' has a generally recognised meaning in ordinary speech. It describes what human beings do, implying that they are free to act and that their action can be judged according to an accepted standard. A parent behaves badly when he ill-treats his child; a politician behaves well when he votes according to his conscience, although his political career may suffer. The assumption in each case is that the person could have acted in the opposite way, and that the action can be measured against a standard such as parental duty or political morality. When applied to systems the term *behaviour* has a different meaning, brought with it from the natural sciences, and used in the less rigorous setting of the social sciences. It implies that a system responds predictably to a particular force or forces (*stimulus* or *stimuli*, to use technical terms). A particular stimulus can have only one outcome, and it is irrelevant to measure it against a moral or other standard. In theory, at any rate, the behaviour of a business system is mechanical: if, for example, the sales system generates an increase in orders, the personnel department organises the increase in man-hours to meet on time the increase; it has behaved as expected. That things do not always happen precisely that way may be due to the human element mentioned earlier.

Loops and feed-backs

Systems mentioned so far have been linked by single straight lines, and parallel lines have not been used. Relationships within a system are often described in this way. Figure 2.5 illustrates the packing system in a chocolate factory: every movement is forward; at no stage is the flow reversed. Contrast this with a domestic gas central-heating system, controlled by a thermostat, as shown in Fig. 2.6.

Under normal conditions, the operation of the controlling system will ensure that the water is kept at 90°F over a long period. The whole system

22 Information Processing for Business Studies

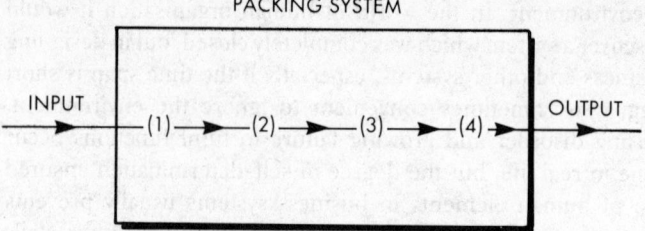

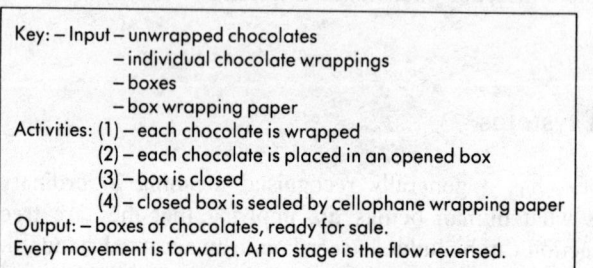

Key: – Input – unwrapped chocolates
– individual chocolate wrappings
– boxes
– box wrapping paper
Activities: (1) – each chocolate is wrapped
(2) – each chocolate is placed in an opened box
(3) – box is closed
(4) – closed box is sealed by cellophane wrapping paper
Output: – boxes of chocolates, ready for sale.
Every movement is forward. At no stage is the flow reversed.

Fig. 2.5 Packing system in a chocolate factory

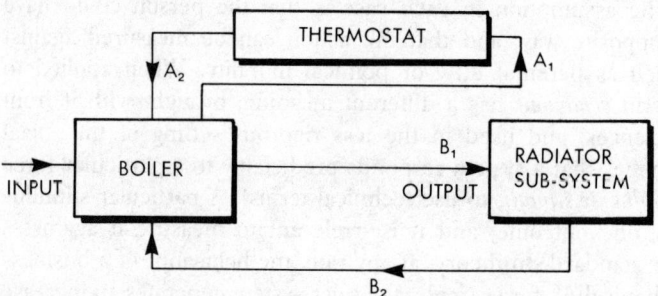

Input: fuel-gas.
Output: water to the radiators.
Thermostat: set at 90°F.
Sequence of events:
1 Whole system is cold, e.g. water throughout is at 50°F.
2 Boiler is switched on and the water is heated.
3 Water flows
       (a) through the radiator sub-system;   (b) through the thermostat sub-system;

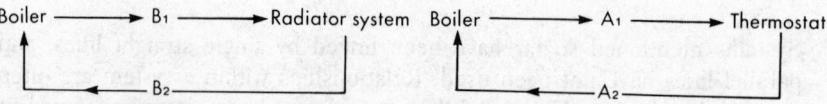

4 As soon as the water temperature rises above 90°F, the control A_2 is triggered off by the thermostat to reduce the gas input. The temperature soon drops to 90°F, the restriction on the gas supply is removed, and the boiler heats the water to 90°F again.

5 If the temperature rises above 90°F the cycle started in 4 is repeated.

Fig. 2.6 Domestic gas central-heating system

is then said to be in *equilibrium*. The term *feed-back* refers to the way in which the thermostat is alerted to the increase in temperature above 90°F. If 3(*b*) describes the main system, then 3(*a*) is a loop on it.

A commercial bank will use a feed-back device to control customer's overdrafts. Suppose a bank's customer, Mr A., is allowed an overdraft of £500 for 1 year on his current account, and at present it is overdrawn by £350. He draws a cheque on it for £125. When this cheque has passed through the clearing system, on its return to the branch his account will be debited, but no further action will be taken. If no further funds reach the account and a second cheque for £80 is drawn upon it, the return of the cheque from clearing will increase the overdraft beyond the limit allowed. Before banks were computerised, the excessive overdraft would come to light when a clerk personally inspected the account. The manager would then notify the customer, ask him to put the matter right and state that unless this were done, the £500 facility would be withdrawn straight away. Since computerisation, one method available is for the whole of a bank's accounts to be monitored by an *exception report* which each day gives details of all accounts of the branch where the overdraft limit has been broken. Chapter 3 will deal with such reports generally.

The systems approach

At first sight, the attention paid to the study of systems when applying computers to the daily work of businesses and organisations may seem hardly justified. The rectangles used to represent systems are simplified, abstract models of real-life situations, which are always more complicated and more concrete than two-dimensional diagrams. A powerful answer to the criticism is that today the majority of computers have been installed, and are being used, through the systems approach. A sophisticated set of techniques has been developed, *systems analysis* and this is practised by a highly trained branch of the computing profession, *systems analysts*. It will require the whole of a later chapter merely to outline that subject, and it seems unlikely that in highly competitive business situations so much money would have been spent on the systems approach if it had been unnecessary.

An underlying reason for the value of the approach is that it compels an objective, scientific and analytical approach to complex situations, which have often developed piecemeal and unsystematically. The smallest group activity will have to be resolved into distinctive elements, and the exact purposes it served will need to be defined. The discipline demanded by such a survey can only be good for the organisation which is surveyed and for the new computing scheme which is to be applied.

A further reason favouring the systems approach is the fact that if a computer is to be used, it is comparatively rare for a single 'machine', as it

24 Information Processing for Business Studies

were, to be known later as the *central processor* to be used alone. It will nearly always need programs to instruct it, and often *peripherals* to feed it and distribute its output. A convenient collective term for these necessities and the people who will use them is 'a computer system'.

Great scope exists, with the aid of logic and mathematics, to explore the theory of systems, and the question of how far this is relevant to the application of computing to business will only be answered as time passes. It is possible that in the development of information-processing techniques, laws relating to oscillation, noise and traffic between systems will be used in the designing of information systems. A basic account of these systems will be given in the next chapter.

Short questions

1   A large firm despatches each day to its customers and others letters and parcels by post.
   (a) Give a brief account of the main activities that this is likely to involve.
   (b) Describing the arrangement as the Postal Despatch system, classify the elements of the system, giving two examples under each heading.

2   Using examples different from those in the text, give an example of how informal human relationships could affect the operation of systems
   (a) in a business organisation;
   (b) in a government or local government organisation.

3   Figure 2.3 represents a situation where communications of various kinds are crossing the interfaces. Give examples of:
   (a) a phone message from B to C;
   (b) a report from D to B;
   (c) an internal memorandum directly from E to C.
What limitation of Fig. 2.3, and similar diagrams, does (c) disclose?

4   Illustrate a hierarchy of systems *either*
   (a) with the UK Cabinet at the top,
or
   (b) with the local agent of a large firm selling by catalogue at the bottom.

5   When new business and organisations come into being, systems are often constructed to overlap.
   (a) Suggest reasons for this.
   (b) What problems are likely to arise through overlapping?

6   Imagine that the last sentence of the section on 'The environment of a system', i.e. 'The environment ... breaks', was read by someone who knew nothing about the environment of systems. Explain in a few sentences how the hotel industry would be affected and why.

7   A public lending library, which has not yet been computerised, issues books to borrowers on a system that retains a ticket for each book lent.

(a) Show the procedure for issuing a book as a line, similar to that shown in Fig. 2.5.

(b) Show a simple loop by considering the complete procedure by which a borrower returns three library books, goes to the shelves and takes out four books. He has, upon entering, a fourth ticket in his pocket.

(c) Show as a diagram the feed-back system of the procedure by which the library notes books which are overdue, notifies borrowers and collects fines.

8 In Fig. 2.7, each rectangle represents a system.

(i)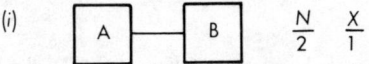

$$\frac{N}{2} \quad \frac{X}{1}$$

(ii)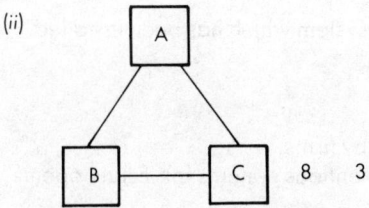

   8   3

(iii)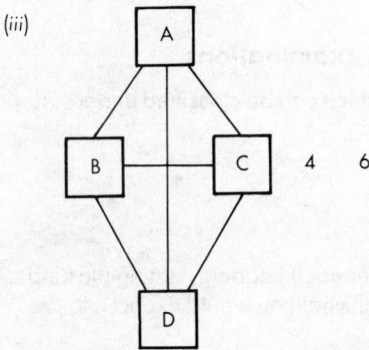

   4   6

Fig. 2.7

(a) What do N and X stand for in the Table?
(b) Add a similar diagram for five systems, stating values for N and X.
(c) If you can see the rule, calculate X in advance for a pattern of five systems. Check with your own diagram.
(d) What statement in the section about the systems approach does this exercise illustrate?

26 Information Processing for Business Studies

Practical work

1 Study a local organisation, e.g. a college or school, a firm, a society or club.
   (a) Draw up a chart showing the main parts in labelled rectangles, connected by straight lines.
   (b) Illustrate the following terms from your study:
      (i) system;
      (ii) sub-system;
      (iii) environment.
   (c) Note changes that have occurred in the organisation, or are planned for.

2 Turn up the 'Computer systems' section of your local *Yellow Pages*. Select a few entries which mention business systems. By enquiries, personal or postal, obtain information to expand what you have learnt from Chapter 2, using the following headings.
   (a) The elements in a typical computer system which has been installed.
   (b) Examples of business systems:
      (i) replaced;
      (ii) newly installed by the firm(s).
   (c) Examples of specialised needs met by firms.
For example, the author's *Yellow Pages* mentions systems for 'Estate agents' and 'PAYE'.
   (d) If possible, provide some details about one special application, investigating 'system' and 'sub-system'.

Questions relevant to BTEC written examinations

1 A business system contains elements which can be classified under headings such as:
   (i) equipment, machinery;
   (ii) human;
   (iii) documents;
   (iv) established procedures.
   (a) Give an example of an element under each heading, stating the kind of business in which it would be found, and what you would expect it to be doing.
   (b) Explain what makes a group of elements into a system, illustrating your answer from answer (a) or otherwise.

2 (a) Explain what is meant by the environment of a system.
   (b) Give examples of changes in the environment of a business, and how a business can respond.
   (c) Give an example of a system in the public sector, and state one way in which its environment would be likely to differ from that of a system in the private sector.

Other examination questions

1 'Knowledge of Systems Theory is essential to the administrator's undertaking of actual systems in an organisation'. Discuss. (IAM – Advanced Methods and Systems paper, Summer 1985)

2 (a) What do you consider to be the significant characteristics of a 'system'?

(b) Describe the relationship of a system with its environment, explaining how you would identify the boundary between the two.

(c) In a manufacturing organisation (which can be regarded as a system) what in your opinion is the relationship of the Chairman and the Managing Director with the environment? (IAM – Advanced Methods and Systems paper, Summer 1984)

3 INFORMATION SYSTEMS

This chapter
- shows how data and information are used in organisations;
- explains what a management report is;
- describes different kinds of report including functional, strategic, tactical, scheduled, *ad hoc* and predictive;
- explains the essentials of a management information system;
- sets out important factors considered in designing management information systems;
- introduces distributed information systems;
- explains how information systems are assessed.

Data and information in organisations

The distinction made between data and information in Chapter 2 rested on whether a given fact informed someone or something. The number '15' as it stands may be merely a piece of data. Add mns and it can become information informing a meteorologist that on a particular day that amount of rain fell at a stated recording station. Figures printed in a special format at the bottom of a bank cheque merely state a number: to a cashier, at the counter, part of the number informs him of the account on which it is drawn; to a sorting machine at the clearing centre, other digits indicate the bank of origin to which the cheque must be returned. In vehicle insurance files, codes of letters and numbers will inform the company's staff of the area and vehicle risk factors used in determining a customer's premium. The data has already become information. When a computing system uses a number of such pieces to produce substantial, ordered statements about a situation, the output is called a report.

The context of a particular statement determines its status. Normally '3.7' would be nothing more than data. In the statement 'The monthly turnover of product A is 3.7', it stands in its own right as information. When combined with corresponding statements about products B and C, a small report has been produced. Statements from a government computer that '3.8 miles of motorway X and 2.4 miles of motorway Y were reconstructed' are best described as information. That these operations cost '£7.6m' and '£6.0m' are also pieces of information. When the computer prints out both statements and adds that the average costs per mile are £2.0m for X and £2.5m for Y, the three assertions make up a small report.

Reports fall into a number of different categories, some of which may overlap, and definitions may vary between writers and countries. But the context in which a report is created and used will usually indicate its real purpose and labelling need not be precise. The next sections will demonstrate the complexity of the problem.

Types of report

Once the gathering of information becomes established in an organisation, reports in the same general format will be issued at regular intervals. Such reports are *scheduled*. Examples are monthly reports on stock levels in manufacturing firms, and the quarterly statements of its current account which a voluntary body arranges to receive from its bank. A single report to meet a particular situation is *ad hoc*. A multiple pharmacy business would, as a matter of urgency, require such a report of its computer when a product had received bad publicity or had otherwise come under suspicion: the report would give information of stocks, and perhaps recent sales from its warehouse and retail branches.

'Management by exception' is a system by which ordinary activities of the organisation are left to junior management, but extraordinary events are brought to the notice of higher management as they may demand decision at this level. In council house administration, for example, the housing manager may be empowered to authorise maintenance of a house up to a stated amount; beyond this, major structural work, for example, must be referred to the housing committee. In most production systems a certain low level of rejects is accepted. An *exception report* would signal any rise above this level, and a system would alert management to the problems.

In long-term planning, an organisation may need information not only from within, but from the environment (using this term in the sense explained in Chapter 2). Information of this kind comes from *background reports*. United Kingdom government policy today is very much affected by the market for British oil. Such a report would give the policies and outputs of other producers, as they affected the international oil market.

Successful planning depends very much upon reading into the future. A firm launching a new product will need to estimate customers' intentions by its own market research, and potential purchasing power by extrapolation of national income statistics. A report covering such data would be *predictive*.

A large organisation will plan at least five years ahead in its policy making. Decisions will concern large-scale capital expenditure, perhaps advance procurement of materials and the undertaking of new enterprises. Reports of these dimensions will be *strategic*, and they will be directed to boards of directors or other forms of top management. The application of strategic decisions by allocating finance in annual budgets, setting production targets and defining related short-term assignments will be sent out in *tactical reports* which it will be the duty of middle management to implement. Daily operations, such as the use of particular machines, the flow of raw materials

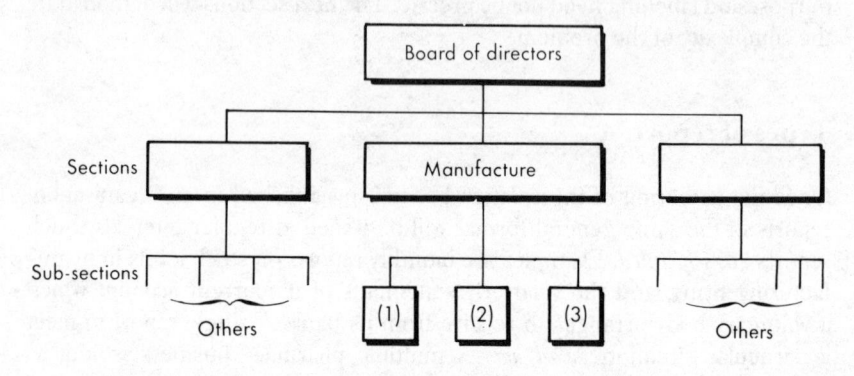

```
                    Board of directors
                           |
        _____|_____
        |                  |                  |
Sections|              Manufacture            |
        |              ____|____              |
Sub-sections  |  |    |    |    |    |  |  |
         \___v___/   (1)  (2)  (3)   \___v___/
           Others                      Others
```

Key:
1 Materials cut and prepared.
2 Furniture assembled.
3 Furniture finished (e.g. varnished, polished, tested and packed).

Fig. 3.1 Pyramidal diagram of an organisation

and semi-finished products, will depend upon information contained in *operational reports* for foremen and others at that level to carry out. Information then in a manufacturing industry will be directed at three different levels: at the top, the instruction will be general, and wide discretion will be allowed in carrying it out. At the bottom, it will be in detail, and the requirements fairly closely defined. The same kind of stratification will be seen in most organisations. The principal officer of a government department will receive reports carrying overall planning well into the future. At executive level the information will relate more to the immediate scene, but allow some administrative discretion. At the lowest level, the report will give such information as the standard rates of social benefits to be paid out, and recent stock levels of official forms, narrowing down the limits within which the official can make decisions. Although the term 'management' denotes decision at high level, all the reports discussed in this paragraph are usually called 'management'.

Most large organisations can be represented as pyramids, the shape being formed from rectangles. A simple example is to include the board of directors in the organisation pictured in Fig. 3.1, and analyse manufacturing activities on the assumption that they could be sub-divided into three distinct operations. The other sections could also be sub-divided, but for convenience in exposition these sub-divisions are omitted.

A report about any of the three sections would be called *departmental*, e.g. about the average time taken for one item to take to pass through the manufacturing stage, or the labour costs required to get a suite from the manufacturing stage into the customer's hands. Reports, similar in scope, could arise from each of sub-sections 1, 2 and 3: for example, the percentage waste when a particular type of wood was used in 1. On the other hand, a report could be about a feature or activity common to one or more sections or sub-sections. An example would be the cost of building maintenance throughout the firm, or the accuracy of documentation as it affected production from the raw-material stage to the finished product. Reports concerned with such matters which stretch beyond sectional or sub-sectional boundaries are called *functional*.

Management information systems

Once a computer is installed in an organisation, with suitable peripherals and programs, a great deal of information is potentially available for management decision-making, although the computing system's main purpose is to serve some routine such as keeping customers' addresses or recording stock or producing weekly pay-slips. But more will be needed if a proper management information system is to operate. The data needed for this specialised purpose will have to be properly collected and stored, and channelled to various levels of management in the most economical way.

A number of detailed points will need to be satisfied. Storage must be adequate and take into account future developments, but not be excessive. The length of time particular items of data need to be stored must be decided. Retrieval and transmission must be convenient and quick. The format of some management reports will be easily designed, without great expertise: the gross profit on a transaction is, for example, easy to calculate. But the design of some reports, and hence the system producing them, may call for expertise. The use of patients' records as an aid to diagnosis in medical research will call for knowledge beyond that found in an ordinary computing department.

In designing a management information system, security and legality considerations are calling for growing care, as Chapter 16 explains.

Distributed information systems

Each system mentioned so far has been based on its own computer with data travelling along one or more circuits to peripherals with which it is linked. Improvements in computer technology have made it possible for an organisation to operate its data-processing and information-processing systems by having a large powerful computer at its centre linked to a smaller computer at each of its outstations. This is a *distributed system*. In suitable cases the arrangement offers saving in time, economy in data storage and convenience in access to documents. A building society, for example, may have a large computer at its head office, linked to smaller computers at its branches throughout the country. Hence, the state of a local customer's account, or information about the unused part of the branch's monthly quota of mortgage funds, can be obtained almost immediately, without reference to the central computer, whereas local data will be fed into the central computer at regular intervals, and the answers to questions of local significance can be obtained through a signal directed to it.

Cost and value of information

The *cost* of a unit of information can be calculated by the same general method used in calculating a unit of a manufactured product or a unit of service. The separate costs of labour, machinery, materials and other items would be taken into account. A fine analysis would also take into account the fact that data produced would be used to varying extents, at different times, in producing information.

Whether a particular piece of information is worth producing depends upon its *value*, and this depends upon a different set of factors.

Suppose a firm already in business is considering launching a new product. It will need to know how many units will be sold at a given price. Its decision will be based on a market research study. This source will be *imperfect information*, as it cannot be certain. The value of the information will depend upon the increase in profits to the firm of a successful launch. In practice, such decisions rest upon calculated probabilities about the status of the information. Many such enterprises are launched upon probabilities of 95 per cent, often rather less. Information which with absolute certainty represented the real state of affairs would be *perfect*. In business, the difficulty of obtaining perfect information is generally recognised.

In such operations as oil-drilling speculation, management's state of knowledge is often far past complete ignorance, but short of perfect information. Its decision then is to balance costs and values and determine the amount of further information it is worth purchasing.

Short questions

1 '*Information* is based on *data* and *reports* are based upon information.'
   (a) Distinguish in your own words between the three italicised terms.

(b) Give an example of a report, and examples of items of data and information you would expect to find in it.

2   Each of the following organisations has a management information system:

(a) an electricity board, which distributes electricity through a defined region of the country;
(b) a PLC renting out TV sets throughout the UK;
(c) a firm making bread and cakes which it sells through 12 shops in the same large town.

Give one example of a report for each organisation, explaining its value to management.

3   Each of the following statements is taken from a different report from a different organisation.

(a) 'By the end of July, 213 houses still needed redecorating, showing a lapse in 45 against scheduled completion.'
(b) 'The directors have set aside £350,000 for the replacement of obsolete vehicles up to 1995.'
(c) 'Profits on West African sales for 1984, before tax, amounted to £109,000.'
(d) 'Shortage of skilled labour in 1984 meant that the expansion of our Shortmoor factory labour force fell short of the scheduled 20 per cent.'

Classify the report from which each statement was taken using *one* of the following categories:

(i) strategic; (ii) tactical; (iii) operational; (iv) not (i), (ii) or (iii).

Give reasons for your choice.

4   A college has a good rate of success in business examinations. Each year the head of department calls for a report on failures.

(a) What general name is given to this report and why?
(b) What data would you expect to find in the report, and from what documents would it be obtained?
(c) What would be the value of such reports?

5   Study Fig. 3.1, labelling the blank sections and suggesting sub-sections below the first and last main sections. Assume that the owners of the factory are considering setting up a management information system.

(a) Give as many examples as possible of how the sections and sub-sections would be concerned.
(b) Give arguments in support of setting up such a system.

6   A firm of car manufacturers sells new cars and new parts, and carries out services through a chain of authorised dealers operating throughout the UK. At the moment, business between dealers and the firm is to some extent computerised. The firm's main office has a computer and keeps files. Data passes between this computer and the dealers through a terminal in each dealer's premises. Explain some disadvantages of the system, what could happen if the manufacturer went over to a distributed system and the advantages of such a change.

Practical work

1 Select a group of at least ten people to co-operate in a data-collecting operation. Preferably they should have a common relationship, in that they attend the same school or college or work at the same place. Systematically collect data from each person under a convenient number of headings:

    Name.
    Address.
    Sex.
    Age (years and months).
    Place of employment or full-time education.
    Whether they own a vehicle, and if so, the type.
    Form of transport they normally take to their place of employment or full-time education – e.g. walk, lift in friend's car.
    Approximate distance travelled.
    How long they have lived at their present address.

Show the data in one large form. Assuming that all the data has been transferred to computer files, suggest how different kinds of useful information can be obtained from it in simple reports, e.g. the relationship between distance and form of transport.

You need not work out the reports in full.

2 Suppose that a firm has moved from another part of the country and built a new factory in your town or district. A number of key workers are to be moved from the old factory to the new one. The firm is prepared to buy outright or help staff to buy suitable modern property. The family units to be rehoused vary from single persons to married families with up to four teenage children. Collect data on property available under such headings as:

    Type – detached, flat, etc.;
    Asking price;
    Distance from factory site;
    Location on local map, e.g. D3;

and other points likely to be of interest to purchasers. Data can be obtained either by collecting sale particulars from local estate agents' offices or from local newspaper advertisements.

(*a*) Set out the data in a single, large table in a form convenient to read.

(*b*) Suppose that all data has been transferred to the firm's computer records.

(*i*) Suggest in outline suitable summaries of the data that could be reported for the guidance of management.

(*ii*) Suggest what changes in the data would be likely to occur, if each year the management updates the data on the table you have drawn up.

(*c*) Illustrate from your exercise that you understand the meaning of 'imperfect information'.

Notes: (A) This project is flexible, in that it could be undertaken by one person, or a few, or a whole class, according to the numbers of properties and agents involved and to the amount of detail collected and recorded for each property.

(*B*) Most property agents will supply free a gridded map of the district they cover.

Questions relevent to BTEC written examinations

1 (*a*) Explain carefully what an information system is.

(*b*) A large company with head office in London makes goods and distributes them in the UK and other countries throughout the world. It has a computerised information system.

Explain the following types of report: (*i*) exception; (*ii*) strategic; (*iii*) operational, illustrating your answer by examples of reports which you would expect the company to produce.

2 (*a*) Distinguish between *fact*, *data*, and *information* when used in a computing context.

(*b*) How are the three terms related?

(*c*) What is the difference between the cost of information and its value?

Other examination questions

1 Computerised management information systems are to be found in both the private and public sector, e.g.
    central and local government;
    nationalised industries;
    non-profit making organisations;
    business organisations manufacturing goods for profit.
In each case it is usual to break the organisation into manageable divisions, so that for example a manufacturing company could be divided into the following areas of operation:
    production and material control;
    marketing and distribution;
    personnel and industrial relations;
    finance and management accounting.
Taking the suggested divisions given for a small manufacturing company, or alternatively taking an organisation of your own choice, you are required:

(*a*) to name three reports that could be produced by the management information system for each division of the organisation;

(*b*) to give four brief explanations as to why information is required by management. (AAT – Data Processing, Dec. 1983)

2 Decision making has often been categorised under the terms strategic, tactical and operational. Analyse and compare the information requirements of each of these three categories. (IAM – Administrative Management paper, Summer 1984)

4 THE ELECTRONIC COMPUTER AND ITS PLACE IN BUSINESS

> This chapter
> - gives examples of simple human calculations, and of earlier mechanical aids;
> - states the basic activity of the electronic computer;
> - explains and illustrates the advantages of the computer.

Human calculations and mechanical aids

It is surprising how many calculations an ordinary person is likely to carry out during the day. If he goes shopping, he will note the price of each article bought, find the total, and pay, either by selecting coins to the exact amount, or tendering a greater amount and checking his change. If he is catching a bus, he will consult the timetable, roughly estimate how long he will take to walk to the bus stop, and what additional time he may need to do other things in the meantime. A journey of any length by car will involve reading from the dashboard how much petrol he has, perhaps judging the distance from a map, and working out the minimum amount of petrol he must have in or put in his tank if he is not to run out. All such calculations are based on the simple arithmetical processes of adding, subtracting, multiplying and dividing, and one other, deciding which is the greater of two numbers. Another ability needed is to remember numbers and to recall them quickly when required. Most people buying a few simple items over the counter of a shop will be able to remember the price of each one and calculate the total amount without using pen and paper.

Except for the occasional human prodigy, human beings have always been limited in the kind of calculations they can perform unaided, and they have invented devices to help them. The abacus, a special bead frame, goes back to about 500 B.C. and is still used in business in the Far East as an alternative to a desk calculator. In the nineteenth century, punched cards were used to control silk looms, to record and present census data, and later to operate mechanical accounting machines. Presently, extensive use was made in business of mechanical, and then electrical, machines, leaving less and less numerical work to be done by manual methods. But it was the development of the electronic computer after the Second World War which produced a revolution for business and other fields of activity in the way in which data was stored and manipulated.

The ability of the electronic computer

Basically, the range of a computer's calculations is no greater than that of a child's, i.e. addition, subtraction, multiplication and division, comparison of numbers, remembering and recalling numbers, and learning methods of handling numbers. Indeed, in some ways a computer is much more clumsy in its methods than an unaided human being. Most young children will almost unhesitatingly arrange the following ages in the correct order of oldest to youngest: 3 yrs, $2\frac{1}{2}$ yrs, 21 yrs, 17 yrs, $33\frac{1}{4}$ yrs, 6 months, 20 yrs, 9 months. The child's approach will be almost instinctive. Although a modern computer can handle the calculation in a split second, a fair comparison must take into account the number of separate instructions that must be given to the computer if it is to receive this data, sort the ages into order and give the correct final list. Readers proficient in writing computer programs in BASIC may care to attempt the exercise and calculate the number of instructions.

A deeper consideration, sometimes lost sight of in discussions of this kind, is that in the final analysis the computer cannot go further in intellectual achievement than the human intelligence which makes, feeds, programs and operates it.

The advantages of using an electronic computer

The reason why electronic computers are so extensively used in business and elsewhere is that they have overwhelming advantages over human beings in speed, capacity and accuracy. How these advantages arise will become clear when the way a computer works is described later in this chapter.

A small computer, properly instructed, can calculate the weekly pay of several hundred workers, update the pay records and print the pay-chits much more quickly and with less manpower than a manually operated system.

Without a computer, an organisation such as a credit-card agency, having thousands of customers, would need a large amount of storage space to record transactions and ensure that a satisfactory service was being maintained and unscrupulous customers were not abusing the system. The complete records of one customer would need at least one form, and one or more large cabinets would be needed to accommodate all the records. Such manual systems usually depend upon a card-index system for convenient work. Chapter 5 will explain why information of this magnitude can occupy much less space when held on computer files. Furthermore, processing the data will be much quicker, and more economical in manpower than with the manual system.

The main cause of errors in clerical processes is human fatigue, with rather fewer mistakes attributable to mechanical failures, e.g. in typewriters and printers. Although computers are prone to error, they are much less prone to fatigue than human beings; and when a computer makes a mistake the error is usually so large as to be immediately obvious. The kind of lapse occasionally found in computer output is to state £310,000, when the amount should be £3.10. The probability of a human-based system stating £3.0 instead of £3.1 is much greater, and the chances of early detection are smaller. Precautions against error are easier to build into computer systems than into ordinary clerical ones. The computer, then, has the advantage of accuracy. In another sense, a computer system is more accurate than the alternative systems. Even the simplest computers can work quickly to a high degree of mathematical accuracy. Suppose that in an industrial costing calculation, the cost of 2 metres of raw material at £7 per metre is required. A human estimator will find the answer, £14, as quickly as a computer. In practice, nicely rounded figures are less likely to occur. Suppose the length is 2.369 metres, and unit price £7.815. An electronic device, calculator or computer, will give an accurate answer £18.513735 much more quickly than an ordinary human being. Furthermore, the computer can be programmed to give the answer to a stated place of decimals. Rounding up to three places, it would be £18.514; rounding down, £18.513; and *truncating*, i.e. cutting off digits beyond the third place, it would be £18.513.

The foregoing properties of a computer enable it to perform extremely complicated calculations very quickly. For example, co-ordinating and timing the activities of the various trades and equipment required in a civil engineering project, e.g. building a bridge, to produce the lowest costs demands techniques of network control. Given a suitable program, a clerk can enter the basic data and obtain an efficient schedule for the whole operation. Direct calculations would normally involve skilled mathematicians and would take very much longer. Business operations often present queueing problems, as in the provision of tills in supermarkets or the flow of raw materials and components to parallel production lines in a factory. A computer can handle the necessary calculations quite readily and be programmed to deal with unusual situations straight away, e.g. the breakdown of a till or an unscheduled slowing down of the supply of a particular component.

Communication to and from a computer is very speedy, and once input and output line are established, very cheap.

Data and information travelling this way are creating a revolution in business communication within firms and organisations and between them. Not only are close networks being set up within the UK, but international lines are being used as well. Chapters 12 and 13 will develop the subject more fully. These computer-centred links are the most advanced of modern methods of communication.

The principles of the electronic computer

The superiority of the electronic computer to earlier machines based on manual and electrical power lies in three related reasons. Whereas electric devices like lights, cookers or vacuum cleaners operate on unbroken flows of electricity along conductors, electronic devices depend upon impulses of electricity travelling at very high speeds. These can be used to convey data much faster, and more economically, than can devices which rely purely on a continuous flow of electricity. Secondly, these impulses can be used to produce microscopic changes in suitable media, in such a way that vast quantities of data can be stored in very small spaces. Thirdly, electronic systems can be adapted to computing techniques by a very simple arrangement called binary coding, which is explained in the next section.

Binary coding

Most business data and information could be expressed by 36 symbols, 26 letters of the alphabet and the 10 digits 0, 1 ... 8, 9. An improvement would be to have upper- and lower-case letters, so that 36 + 26 symbols would be required, i.e. 62. It would be even more useful to add punctuation marks (., ?, etc.), mathematical instructions (+ −, etc.) and common business symbols such as £, %. But each time a different element of data was put into the computer, it would need to be transformed into a distinctive electronic representation, and at the output, the electronic representations would have to be transferred into letters, digits and symbols forming a readable message. The use of a binary code simplifies the construction and operation of the computer. Instead of having 36, or even more, symbols together with the resulting complication in transformation and re-transformation, the data can be processed with two.

These two are in fact the digits '0' and '1'. If they are used with two places to be filled, four different arrangements are possible, as shown:

Place I	*Place II*
0	0
0	1
1	0
1	1

40 Information Processing for Business Studies

The use of three places doubles the number of different permutations:

Place I	Place II	Place III
0	0	0
0	0	1
0	1	0
0	1	1
1	0	0
1	0	1
1	1	0
1	1	1

The addition of one more place always doubles the number of permutations. The application of the rule is shown in Table 4.1. Hence, filling five different places with different arrangements of 0 and 1 would give a simple code allowing messages in any of the 26 letters of the English alphabet to be processed, with the possibility of using a total of six digits or other symbols as well.

Table 4.1

No. of places, N	No. of permutations	$= 2^N$
2	4	$= 2^2$
3	8	$= 2^3$
4	16	$= 2^4$
5	32	$= 2^5$
6	64	$= 2^6$

The digits 0 and 1 of the binary system are at separate points on the computer medium. Each point is *bistable*, i.e. it can be in one or two states electronically, and given a suitable impulse the state can be reversed. It can be at 0 and then changed to 1, or 1 and then changed to 0. Analogous changes which show how the 0 and 1 alternatives are used in computing are represented in Fig. 4.1.

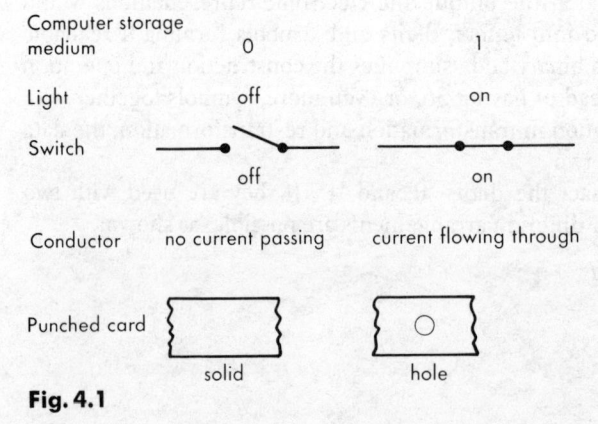

Computer storage medium	0	1
Light	off	on
Switch	off	on
Conductor	no current passing	current flowing through
Punched card	solid	hole

Fig. 4.1

Decimal notation to binary

Numbers used in business life are usually in *decimal* or *denary* notation, i.e. based on 10. Suppose 47 articles have been sold, and the data has to be entered into a computer. Using 10 and indices, the number as it stands is:

$$\begin{array}{cc} 10^1 & 10^0 \\ \hline 4 & 7 \end{array}$$

Checking, using the fact that $10^1 = 10$, $10^0 = 1$ the number is

$$\begin{aligned} 4 \times 10 &= 40 \\ 7 \times 1 &= \underline{7} \\ &47 \end{aligned}$$

Successive division by 2 and noting remainders gives the binary equivalent:

$$\begin{aligned} &2)\underline{47} \\ &2)\underline{23} + 1 \\ &2)\underline{11} + 1 \\ &2)\ \underline{5} + 1 \\ &2)\ \underline{2} + 1 \\ &\underline{1} + 0 \end{aligned}$$

In binary form, then, 47 is written 101111. Checking gives:

$$\begin{array}{cccccc} 2^5 & 2^4 & 2^3 & 2^2 & 2^1 & 2^0 \\ \hline 1 & 0 & 1 & 1 & 1 & 1 \end{array} \quad \text{or} \quad \begin{aligned} 1 \times 2^5 &= 32 \\ 0 \times 2^4 &= 0 \\ 1 \times 2^3 &= 8 \\ 1 \times 2^2 &= 4 \\ 1 \times 2^1 &= 2 \\ 1 \times 2^0 &= \underline{1} \\ &47 \end{aligned}$$

Use of the binary code makes for simplicity, but can be extravagant in storage space. Using six places for each original *character*, i.e. letter, or digit or symbol, would mean that a five-letter word would require $5 \times 6 = 30$ places in the computer or storage medium.

An economy can be made by using 8 as the basis of the first conversion, then re-applying binary. For example, 4235 is converted to the octal system as follows:

8)<u>4235</u>
8)<u>529</u> + 3
8)<u> 66</u> + 1
8)<u>   8</u> + 2
    <u>1</u> + 0

8^4	8^3	8^2	8^1	8^0
1	0	2	1	3

Checking as before gives:

$1 \times 8^4 = 4096$
$0 \times 8^3 = 0$
$2 \times 8^2 = 128$
$1 \times 8^1 = 8$
$3 \times 8^0 = \underline{3}$
4235

But from this calculation, the new digits 2, 3, 4 and 5 would need separate coding, and other calculations could produce 6 and 7 as well. This range of octal digits is expressed in binary as shown in Table 4.2.

Table 4.2

Octal		Binary	Check
0	→	000	0 + 0 + 0
1	→	001	0 + 0 + 1
2	→	010	0 + 2 + 0
3	→	011	0 + 2 + 1
4	→	100	4 + 0 + 0
5	→	101	4 + 0 + 1
6	→	110	4 + 2 + 0
7	→	111	4 + 2 + 1

Converting 1, 0, 2, 13 with Table 4.2 gives a final form of

001, 000, 010, 001011

This is the *binary coded octal system*.

An even more powerful system is based on 16. Remainders of 0–15 are possible; 0–9 can be expressed by extending Table 4.2 as follows:

Hexadecimal		Binary
8	→	1000
9	→	1001

using one more space. The numbers 10–15 are presented by the letters A–F respectively, which in turn can be converted into binary. This system is known as the *hexadecimal coded binary system*.

The output of a computer, if it is to be directly read (e.g. a bank account balance or the address of a customer), will be decoded. The sequence of events then will be:

(1)	(2)	(3)	(4)
Data in readable form	→ Binary or binary-based code	→ Processing	→ Decoding into readable form

In business situations, data may already be in coded form 2 before reading; for example, the name of a product advertised in a mail-order catalogue may be represented by a short unique combination of letters and digits, and corresponding decoding occurs on output.

Essential parts of a computer

In Fig. 4.2, A, B, C and D constitute what is usually called the computer, or more accurately, the central processor. E consists of a device or devices for putting data into the computer, and F for outputting it. A later chapter will describe these in some detail. Data will enter the internal access store C. Operations of the kind mentioned on pp. 48–49 will be performed on

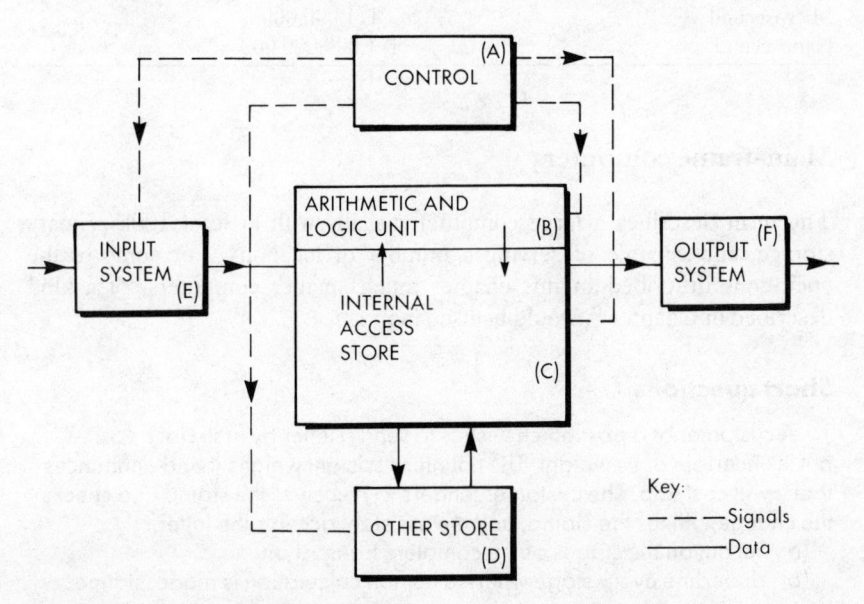

Fig. 4.2 Essential parts of a computer

it in accordance with a program already put into this store and carried out in B. D provides extra storage capacity and its precise role will be explained in Chapter 5. The operation of the whole system is controlled by A, usually a combination of automatic and human-operated controls.

Computing terms and measurements

The binary digits, 0 and 1, are called *bits*. A group of eight bits is called a *byte*, reflecting the fact that many computers work on an eight-bit code representing 256 different characters. A computer will be designed to work with a combination of bits of set length known as the *word length*. Eight bits is a common length, but larger computers use 12 or 16, and some modern computers can work in more than one word length, at the discretion of the operator. *Kilobyte* is a measure of the memory capacity of a computer. It equals 2^{10} bits = 1024 bits, so that a 16k store would be 16,384 bits. An even larger measure is a *megabyte*, a memory capacity of 2^{20} bits = 1,048,576 bits.

Speeds used in computing are so great that they are expressed in very small divisions of a second, in accordance with Table 4.3.

Table 4.3

Unit	Fraction of section	Symbol
Millisecond	1/1,000	ms
Microsecond	1/1,000,000	μs
Nanosecond	1/1,000,000,000	ns

Main-frame computers

The term describes a large computer, usually with at least 100k primary storage, and capable of serving a number of locations. For some of the operations described in this chapter much smaller computers, of a kind described in Chapter 8, would be used in practice.

Short questions

1 A customer at a post office wishes to send a letter by first-class post, but is uncertain of its weight. The counter assistant weighs it and announces that it will cost 23p. The customer tenders £1, receives the stamp and checks the change, affixes the stamp, and the assistant accepts the letter.
   (a) Set out all the stages of the complete transaction.
   (b) Underline every stage where a human calculation is made, stating by whom it is made.

Fig. 4.3 Main-frame computers

2   Suppose three different ages are held in a computer, as follows:

A	B	C
7 yrs	2 yrs	19 yrs

The ages are to be placed in order of size, the greatest in A, the next in B and the smallest in C, using the computer's power to compare two ages and state which is greater. It starts:

1   Compare A and B. $A > B$, therefore leave B.
2   Compare B and C. $B < C$, therefore move B to C, and C to B.
   (a) Complete the instructions until the ages are in the right order.
   (b) Perform a similar operation on the following:

R	S	T	U
2 yrs	13 yrs	0 yrs	18 yrs

Note: $>$ means 'greater than' and $<$ 'less than'.

3   Explain in your own words the two different senses in which the word 'accuracy' is used.

4   Explain the differences between a purely electrical device and an electronic one, using different examples from those given in the chapter.

5   A firm with about 300 customers prepares all its invoices by hand. Explain the advantages which using a computer would bring.

6 Calculate:
  (a) the decimal equivalent of 01101 (which is in binary);
  (b) the binary equivalent of 53 (which is in decimal).

7 A computer store holds a number expressed in binary coded octal as

   110   001   101.

  (a) What original number in denary does it represent?
  (b) Why would octal be used instead of binary?

8 Study Fig. 4.2 and the related text. From examples given in the text, or otherwise, show how the working of a computer corresponds with that of a human being performing an everyday calculation without mechanical or electronic aids.

9 Given that the speed of light is 3×10^8 m/s, express it in terms of m/ms, m/µs, and m/ns.

Practical work

1 Collect practical examples of coding, other than binary. Some examples are to be found on

library books,
driving licences,
income tax documents,
catalogues,
travel agents' brochures, and
banking procedures,

and others are encountered by most people in everyday life.
  (a) Explain what each code signifies and the advantage in using it.
  (b) Select your two simplest examples. Outline the way they would be converted into binary, and state why.

2 Find a firm or organisation which does not use a computer, and ask permission to study it. Examples could be a club, school, office, shop, estate agent, etc.
  (a) Prepare a brief account of the office procedures occurring and the information, if any, which the management is systematically obtaining from it.
  (b) Write a convincing report for the benefit of management explaining the advantages a computer would bring.

  Or: Answer (a) and (b) for a garage which repairs and services cars, and sells new cars, petrol and accessories.

Questions relevant to BTEC written examinations

1 Explain what an electronic computer is, and the part played by the binary code in working it.

2 (a) Draw a sketch showing the main parts of a main-frame computer.
   (b) The computer performs the following calculations:

   A 2 × 3 = 6
   B 35 ÷ 7 = 5
   C A + B = 11

Showing the paths of data thus ─▶─ and of instructions ─ ▶ ─ explain the way the computer undertakes the calculations.

Other examination questions

1 Discuss the main functions of a CPU. (IDP — Part I, June 1985)

2 Discuss, with the aid of examples, the advantages of using computers rather than manual clerical systems. (IMS – Foundation Studies, Computers and Computing, Nov. 1985)

3 A computer consists of a number of functional elements.
   (a) Describe each of these elements.
   (b) Show, with the aid of a diagram, how they are related.
   (c) What type of printer would be most suitable for each of the following situations?
      (i) The pay-roll department of a large firm.
      (ii) A solicitor's office.
      (iii) A drawing office.
(RSA – June 1985)

5 THE STORAGE OF DATA

> This chapter
> - explains why information processing data is stored;
> - describes the different kinds of storage media, and the devices used for storage;
> - introduces and explains various technical terms used in these accounts.

The need to store data

Earlier chapters have described an information-processing system as a single line from left to right, with data entering a computer where it is processed and put out on the other side. If the flow were at the same speed throughout the processing system, then no special arrangements would be needed. In practice this would rarely be the case, as generally speaking the data can be processed in the computer at a greater rate than it can be taken in or put out. Furthermore, storage is needed in the computer itself, for reasons to be explained.

Immediate access store (IAS)

This is the name given to the large store which is built into the computer itself. Data can only be processed if instructions await its arrival, and these need to be in the store already. They control movement of data and signals to and from the arithmetic and logic unit along the connecting lines shown in Fig. 4.2.

As main-frame computers developed, the main stores used consisted of sets of ferrite rings. Each ring, by the passage of an electronic current in a nearby conductor, could be magnetised to represent a binary digit, say 0; reversing the current produced the opposite kind of magnetism which would represent the other binary digit, 1. As the electronic techniques used in computing improved, the limitations of these *cores*, as they were called, became increasingly obvious. The transferring of data from one location to another is known as *reading*, and reading from a ferrite core destroys that item of data; generally, it will need to be replaced, so that processing is slower than it is with other systems of storage where data is not destroyed by reading. Ferrite cores are heavy and need assembling, so that construction is expensive compared with stores which are made by engraving or printing on special surfaces.

Backing store

The store just described is an integral part of the computer. Its contents are directly available in the operations mentioned. The 'other store' shown in Fig. 4.2 extends the storage space available for data, but the contents are not directly accessible: they need to be transferred to the IAS for operations. It is called an auxiliary or backing store, and of course data can be put into it from the processor.

Fig. 5.1 Magnetised disk loaded into its drive

Magnetised disks

The principle just described, that of opposite magnetic states being used to represent 0 and 1 respectively, has been much more conveniently adopted in modern storage methods using magnetic media. This consists of a thin layer of magnetisable material spread on rigid or flexible plastic. On the surface are minute magnetisable dots. The surface is moved rapidly and the data is written on to it or read from it by combined read/write heads.

The simplest example is shown in outline in Fig. 5.1 (p. 49). The disk resembles a gramophone record with rings on the surface which are separate but packed closely together. The disk is rotated rapidly by a *drive* and the data transferred through a retractable arm.

A more elaborate store consists of a vertical stack of 11 disks of equal size, fitting a single spindle and served by a set of ten pick-up heads, the lowest and the highest disk surfaces not being used for storage.

Fig. 5.2 Floppy disk

The storage of data 51

In some systems, the disks are fixed; in others they are removable, which has the advantage that a particular disk can be physically removed, used at a distance and returned for further processing.

Floppy disks are extensively used these days, especially with small computers. They are small, convenient for carrying and protected by an envelope, data being transferred through a gap. They are relatively cheap and, for their size, have a great storage capacity.

Fig. 5.3 Winchester disk in its drive (*by courtesy of GEC Computers Ltd*)

A modern development is the *Winchester disk*. It is made of metal, and has much greater storage capacity than earlier types of disk. As it revolves at high speed, data can be transferred very rapidly. A precision-made device, it is kept enclosed, so that data is well protected. Some models have more than one disk on the same shaft. (See Fig. 5.3.)

Other magnetised media

Magnetic drums were extensively used as backing stores of earlier computers. The data was stored in the magnetisable material of the curved surface, and was written on to or read from the surface by fixed heads which scanned circular tracks. Although great storage capacity was offered, data transfer only occurred when the item was opposite the head, so that the process was comparatively slow. However, at that time great speed was not essential in movement between the main and the backing store.

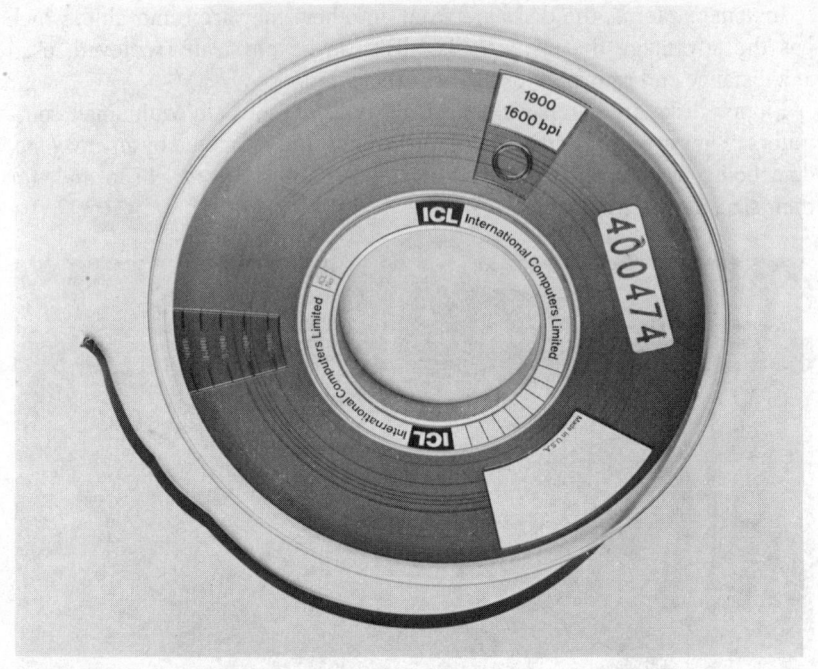

Fig. 5.4a Magnetic tape

Magnetic tape has been widely used for some time in sound recorders. In a similar way it can be used to record data. The tape is coated with magnetisable material, and the data is recorded on magnetisable spots placed on tracks, from six to eight in number, running along the tape. The tracks are divided by gaps across the length of the tape. Smaller and cheaper devices on a similar principle to magnetic tape are *magnetic cassettes*, similar in form to sound cassettes, and *magnetic cartridges*. The cartridge, like the cassette, is a sealed device, but it consists of a single loop of tape wound in one circle.

Data can be stored on *plastic cards*, used singly or kept in groups in special cartridge holders. At one time they were widely used in computer-based accounting machines, and for input in early desk-top computers. In data and information processing they have been largely superseded by other methods, but data is still being stored on cards for security passes, borrowers' library tickets and other purposes.

Paper tape and punched cards

Before the invention of electronic computers, paper tape was used as input and output of telex machines. Data was shown as patterns of holes along

Fig. 5.4b Magnetic tape drive

tracks running the length of the tape, each row of dots at right angles to the run indicating a character. Paper tapes were employed in earlier days in computing, but are little used today. The same is largely true of punched cards—patterns of holes punched on cards of standard design.

In both types of media, when adapted to computing, the data pattern was sensed by the fact that an electrical circuit would be completed when the holes passed over prearranged points on the reading device, but would be broken when paper or cardboard reached it. Punched cards are still being made, probably because so many computers and systems were based on them in the past. But paper and cardboard devices are much inferior to modern storage media. They are slow in every way, inconvenient in use, expensive in manpower and very much subject to wear and tear and the inaccuracies caused by prolonged use.

Semi-conductor storage

A semi-conductor is a substance which can conduct electricity or offer significant resistance to it according to some physical condition such as temperature. This useful property can be further developed in electronic devices by *'doping'*, the process of adding small measured quantities of impurities. Some conductors can be employed to store large quantities of data in remarkably small areas. Chips of *silicon* doped with boron, phosphorus or other elements have been extensively used in this way. Highly sophisticated technology is needed in the manufacture of silicon chip stores. The raw silicon must be sliced, patterns must be etched on, the material doped and a tiny layer of metal applied. Chapter 8 shows a further application for silicon chips in computer construction.

Bubble storage

Another form of storage still being developed depends upon manufacturing techniques which use a thin layer of garnet, into which very tiny cylinder-shaped bubbles can be placed. Each bubble is magnetised in the opposite way to its environment, and the bubbles can be moved rapidly round by magnetic fields created from outside. The presence of a bubble indicates '1' and its absence '0'. However, development has not come up to first expectations, as techniques for driving the bubbles are not as efficient as the storage facilities themselves.

Laser storage

The new term 'laser' is an acronym for Light Amplification by Stimulated Emission of Radiation. Light, as encountered in everyday life, consists of a combination of various wavelengths. Light travelling in a laser beam has a coherent predetermined wavelength pattern, giving it properties for the transmission of data much superior to those of ordinary light. A controlled laser beam falling on a special surface can produce microscopic changes which can be used for data storage. Laser technology is making other contributions to computing which will be described later in Chapters 6, 12 and 13.

Other developments

Improved storage techniques are being constantly sought in computing techniques. Two of interest are the charged couple device, in which electrical charges, controlled by electrical fields, are used instead of magnetic bubbles as described above. Still undergoing research are *Jophenson junctions*, which depend upon the very great increase in conductivity that silicon and certain other substances undergo when very low temperatures are reached. Although knowledge of these techniques is not required by ordinary information-processing syllabuses, readers seeking further information are referred to the bibliography on p. 186.

Specialised terms relating to store

A *buffer store* is the one which holds data which awaits processing, and it is often an integral part of a device. The term *memory* is sometimes equivalent to store, but it is more correct to confine its use to that part of a computer which holds the program and data. *Register* is an even narrower term and refers to a part of a memory holding data or instructions servicing a defined purpose: the storage is usually temporary. The term *read only memory* (ROM) has come into increasing use as chips have been developed as stores. The information is placed in the memory when the chip is manufactured. One example is operating instructions. They will always be required in their original form, and cannot be altered.

Access to stores

Readers using sound tape records will know that to hear a passage in the middle of a piece of music, the tape must be run up to that point, i.e. the sequence of notes (and perhaps silences) must be followed. The access is *sequential*. This disadvantage is suffered by magnetic tapes, already described. In a *random access store*, the required data is located without the need for going through everything that preceded it. Where data is recorded on a disk, the moving arm goes straight to the circular groove containing the required piece of data, transferring it as soon as the rotation brings it within range of the reading head.

The performance of stores

Storage devices vary greatly in their capacity and working principles, and rapid changes are occurring in this branch of computing technology. A number of factors decide which device is used in a particular situation. Speed of storage is an obvious one. A random access device will locate required data more quickly than a serial one, but speed of transfer must be taken into account as well. Another factor is storage capacity in relationship to physical size. Some kinds of store, such as semi-conductors, are *volatile*: the record of the data disappears when the device is switched off. Paper tape is obviously not volatile. Where a store is not volatile, stored data may deteriorate gradually or be corrupted by external magnetic influence.

Miniaturisation

With the coming of the silicon chip and other devices, the trend in storage techniques is to pack more and more data into less and less space. The aim is not merely to reduce bulk. The concentration involved means that movement of data is speeded, power consumption is less and exposure to corruption is reduced.

Short questions

1   A large firm has a computer-produced price list covering 50 different items, which it sends to customers. It updates the list every three months. Producing the list for 1 March 1985 involves:
  (*i*)   deleting three products no longer sold;
  (*ii*) adding two new products;
  (*iii*) increasing the prices of size products by 4 per cent.
  (*a*) Describe in a series of simple statements the processing to be performed by the computer to produce the March updated price list.
  (*b*) Describe the parts to be played by the IAS and the backing store in this processing.

2   Name types of store using magnetised media, and explain in your own words how they record data.

3   Why has disk storage taken several different forms?

4   Explain why:
  (*a*) a variety of storage devices are to be found in modern computing;
  (*b*) changes are still occurring.

Practical work

1   By enquiries at local shops and by studying newspaper advertisements, collect information about data and program storage for the following:
  (*a*) home computers;
  (*b*) small business computers.

Also, collect information about
(c) video tapes;
(d) sound recording tapes.
What points made in this chapter are illustrated by your survey?

2   By consulting an encyclopaedia and other books in a good library, obtain information about earlier computers, and prepare notes on the methods of storage used. Explain why these methods have been replaced.

Questions relevant to BTEC written examinations

1   (a) Describe for each of the following a form which each store can take, and the separate purposes served by each store:
   (i) the immediate access store of a computer;
   (ii) the backing store of a computer;
   (b) explain why a computer system is likely to include other types of store, giving two examples.

2   (a) Explain how the capacity of a computer store is usually measured.
   (b) Explain other points, besides capacity, which are taken into account in number and types of stores to be put into new computer system. You should give brief definitions of terms such as 'buffer', 'distributed', etc., which you may use.

Other examination questions

1   Describe the characteristics and operation of a magnetic disk unit. (CGLI – Data Processing Fundamentals paper, June 1985)

2   (a) Discuss the need for backing stores in computer systems.
   (b) Describe three different types of magnetic storage, and explain the main advantages of each. (IMS – Application and Use of Computers paper, Nov. 1984)

6 INPUT AND OUTPUT METHODS

> This chapter
> - explains the purpose of input and output devices in processing;
> - describes the working principles of
>   punched media,
>   magnetic tapes,
>   magnetic cards,
>   magnetic ink and optical recognition systems,
>   Kimball tags,
>   light pens,
>   digitising devices,
>   voice and speech output, and
>   keyboard entry;
> - summarises forms of output;
> - describes the working principles of visual display units;
> - describes the main types of printers used in computing, and the criteria for selecting a printer;
> - describes output by
>   microfiche,
>   synthesised speech, and
>   punching machines.

Purpose of input and output devices

Diagrams and explanations given earlier show that computers receive data from the outside world, process it and then return it. As computing has developed, a variety of devices for doing this have been invented and used. Some are going out of date. Each kind in use has a particular purpose for which it is best suited. In general the variety of ways in which data can be put into a computer and taken from it is increasing and technology is becoming faster and more efficient.

Punched media

Punched cards and paper tape were described earlier as storage media. Special devices needed to read them, i.e. to transfer the data to the computer for processing, act on the principle that the passage of a punch-hole at a particular point in a reading device completes an electrical circuit which is broken again when solid cardboard or tape follows. Signals in accordance with the pattern of holes then travel to the computer, entering as data or instructions.

Magnetic tapes

They are read by a machine which rapidly transfers the tape from one reel to another past a rapid reading device. For high-speed reading, either side of the device is a loop of the tape in a vacuum to reduce the impact and risk of snapping when the tape is being taken up by the drive.

Magnetic cards

In early desk-top and business computers, cards containing data or programs were inserted by hand in a slot in a machine and a rolling mechanism slowly took them through past a reading head. In a later development, a required card was taken mechanically from a stack inserted into the computer and returned to the pack after the transfer of data.

An up-to-date version is the modern credit card, known as a *badge*. On each card is data in two different forms, the user's name and reference number in embossed plastic, and a magnetic stripe on the back containing other data which can be electronically read. The card is used by being pushed into a machine and read by rollers. Other kinds of computer readable cards include those which act as keys to open electronic security devices.

Magnetic ink characters

The set of numbers at the bottom of a cheque identify the bank, the branch and the customer's account. They are printed in magnetic ink, so that data can be transferred by a MICR (magnetic ink character recognition system).

⑈⑈ ⑴⑆⑆ ⑴⑆⑥⑈⑈ ⑷⑆⑈⑈⑆⑷⑆⑨⑴⑈ ⑸⑴⑴⑷⑨⑨⑦⑶⑈⑈

Fig. 6.1 Magnetic ink characters

In such systems specially printed upper-case letters and symbols are used for documents outside banking as well.

Optical recognition systems

Unlike systems which use magnetic ink, these transfer data written in ordinary ink, but generally adaptations of normal printing fonts are used. The data can therefore be read with ease by people using the original documents and by the computer. The transfer is made by reading through a special light source, the outlines of the characters being a stimulus for corresponding responses in the computer or storage device. An adaptation of the method is the *optical mark reading system*. It is widely used for the transfer of numerical data from batches of similar documents. Alphabetical data of a limited kind can be conveniently transferred by the method, but it is not suitable where all 26 letters are employed. Suppose a number of up to five digits has to be transferred. On the recording document will be printed five columns of digits 0–9, and the person recording a particular figure, e.g. the number of items of X held in stock, will mark in pencil the required digit. The diagram (Fig. 6.2) shows a count of 2,307 items.

```
0  0  0  ∅  0
1  1  1  1  1
2  ∤  2  2  2
3  3  ∦  3  3
4  4  4  4  4
5  5  5  5  5
6  6  6  6  6
7  7  7  7  ∤
8  8  8  8  8
9  9  9  9  9
```

Fig. 6.2   Optical mark reading system

The system has a variety of applications, e.g. in time-sheets, multiple-choice examinations and for reading gas and electricity meters. When billing customers, in a fully computerised system the computer may produce an original form, e.g. a form giving a gas customer's name, address and account number and a set of digits for the meter-reading. The bill can be produced by returning the completed form to the computer. This is an example of a *turn-around document*.

In principle an *optical recognition system* could be devised to read ordinary hand-writing. Such are the variations between different people's hand-writing, and within one person's writing, that systems which could input data written in script are not commercially viable. However, some progress has been made, and some systems will put in data in capital letters to standard size and pattern.

Bar codes

Figure 6.3 shows an example of data in bar-code form, a method which is widely used today as input data. A common example is labels used to identify products for sale and their manufacturers. In a computerised supermarket, the data will be read at the check-out by a low-power laser beam, processed from a stored price record, to appear as a price item on a line of the customer's bill.

Fig. 6.3 Bar code

In a computerised lending library, a bar-code label will appear inside the cover of each book, and each reader will be identified by a unique bar code on his plastic ticket. The two codes will be electronically brought together at the issue desk when a book is borrowed or returned.

Each code is based on the position and width of each black band, unit width corresponding with binary 1, and each white band, with a unit representing binary 0.

Kimball tags

These are used on ready-made garments in shops to record sales. A special label is fixed to the unsold garment. Data about it is recorded in a pattern

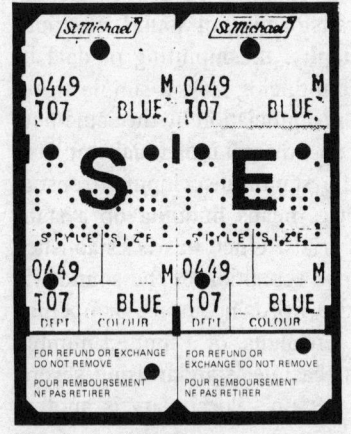

Fig. 6.4 Kimball tag

of small holes on a detachable part of the tag. When the sale occurs, the coded part of the tag is torn off at a perforation, and kept with other parts to be processed either on the spot or to be sent for processing elsewhere.

Light pens

These are electronically sensitive devices used for reading bar codes and other kinds of data. They are shaped like a pen, with a *transistor*, a special kind of chip device, at its point. When held over a patch of light, an electronic impulse occurs which can be read by the computer as data. (See Fig. 6.5.) Another use is in input systems designed to put in plans and other graphic material. The pen is run over the lines to be transferred. (See Fig. 6.6.)

Digitising techniques

These are used to put in patterns of lines, e.g. rectangles of given sizes or circles of given radii. The principle is that positions on a surface, as on a graph, can be defined by numbers. For example, (2, 7) means a point fixed 2 units along the x- or horizontal axis and 7 units along the y- or vertical axis. The computer can be instructed to print in a point or points and to draw lines of defined length, shape and direction from them.

Voice and speech input

Although a particular sound can be uniquely defined by the wavelength and amplitude of the vibrations, and the transforming of sound vibrations into electronic impulses presents little difficulty, the inputting of data by voice and speech presents problems. In pronouncing, say, a simple word, different people will differ significantly, and pronunciation by the same person will vary on different occasions. Talking speeds and individual emphasis are among the factors to be considered. To standardise input to ensure 100 per cent accuracy in computer response means building up a standardised input based on a large number of trials. Once this is established and put into the computer, a sufficiently close repetition of the sound will produce the required result, e.g. printing the word in output, or opening a door. Hence, inputting in vocal form the ten digits, or a limited number of words such as 'stop', 'go' or 'return', is feasible; standardising several thousand words which make up a normal person's vocabulary is another matter.

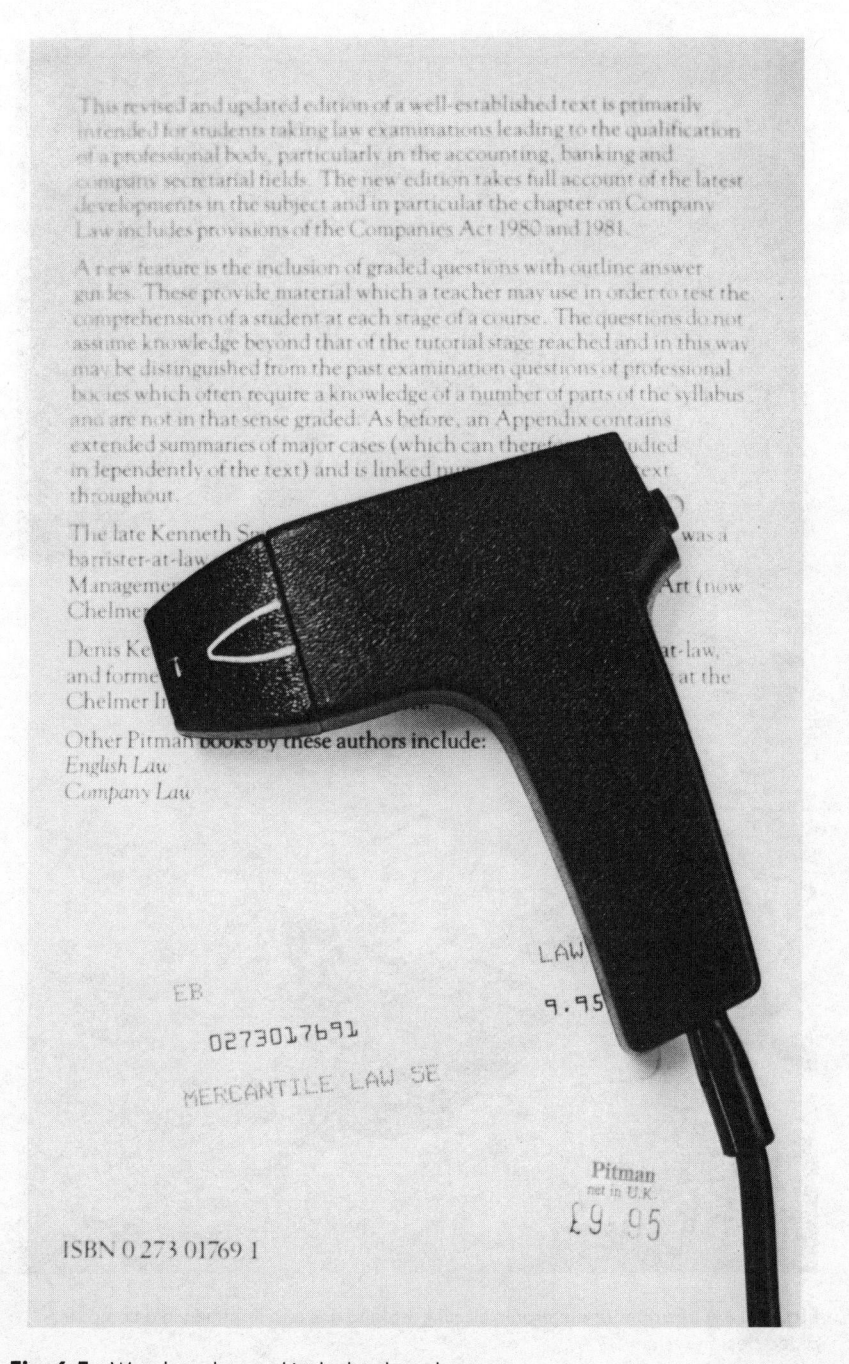

Fig. 6.5 Wand reader used in the book trade

Fig. 6.6 A designer of electronic circuits making use of a light pen in a computer-aided design system

Keyboard entry

Data can be entered on a keyboard similar to that found on an ordinary typewriter. A *key-to-tape* machine receives data into a buffer store and when a complete record is entered, it is transferred to a magnetic tape. A *key-to-disk* machine transfers data to a hard disk, and a variation of the machine transfers the data to *floppy disks*. Keyboard entry devices can be used independently in *stand-alone* form, or in systems where more than one *key-station* feeds a single tape or disk.

Fig. 6.7 Keyboard to disk device

Forms of output

The output of a computer can take various forms. It can be seen on an illuminated screen, printed out, heard as a sound, passed on to another computer, or stored for future use. Another possibility, met more frequently in industrial rather than commercial applications, is that it can control a process: for example it can regulate temperature or the strength of a solution, or remove a defective component from a production line. The devices described below all have commercial uses, but some have industrial and scientific applications as well.

Visual Display Units (VDUs)

A *VDU* resembles a TV screen and displays in an illuminated picture the output from a home computer, a business computer, a main-frame computer or a *microcomputer* (to be defined in Chapter 8). Some VDUs are an integral part of the computer they serve, some are independent, and some are part of other devices, e.g. the key-input machines already mentioned.

Fig. 6.8 Visual display unit

The screen will show figures, words, graphs, diagrams and pictures according to its design and the requirements of the system in which it is used. Most VDUs have been based on emission from a *cathode-ray tube* upon a curved screen. A modern alternative uses *light-emitting diodes* and liquid-crystal displays, with the advantages of greater compactness and economy in power consumption. Some VDUs have facilities for using colour, shading areas in, projecting lines and indicating the last point of data entry by blinking.

Input and output methods **67**

VDUs have a number of direct simple business applications. In the bank manager's office, the state of a customer's account can be shown at the press of a button. A librarian can throw on a screen the titles of books out to a particular borrower. When applied to the storage of car spares, a mechanic can obtain not only the code number of a particular component, but a picture of it, so that he can judge its suitability for the job without undue searching. In some systems, the process of obtaining detailed information through a VDU simulates holding a conversation, and the process is called *interrogation*.

Printers

The commonest form which business output takes is the printed record. A variety of printers have evolved, and techniques are still developing to

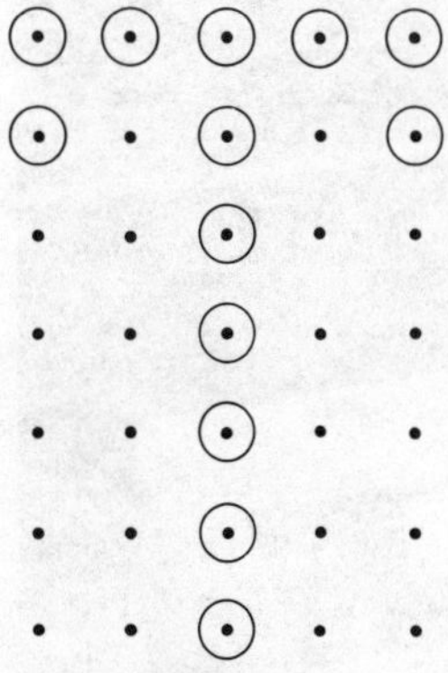

⊙ ⊙ ⊙ ⊙ ⊙
⊙ · ⊙ · ⊙
· · ⊙ · ·
· · ⊙ · ·
· · ⊙ · ·
· · ⊙ · ·
· · ⊙ · ·

Fig. 6.9

make printing speeds match those of input and processing. *Serial printers*, like office typewriters, print one character at a time until one line is completed, and then return to the beginning of the next. In a *daisy-wheel printer*, each character occurs on the circumference of a circle at the end of a 'spoke', lying along the line of a radius. The wheel moves across the paper and the required characters strike inked ribbon against the paper. In *golf-ball printers* the heads lie on the surface of a sphere and the spokes radiate from the centre.

In printing technology, the term *font* describes the style of a set of characters, a quality which will be apparent to the ordinary reader. The printers described above use *solid font* because continuous lines indicate characters. This contrasts with *dot-matrix printing*, which uses a rectangular group of needles. Electronic impulses select and push against the ribbon those required to print a particular character. The setting of a 5×7 matrix for printing 'T' is shown in Fig. 6.9.

Solid-font printers rely on impact, i.e. printing involves a mechanical, striking action. Some matrix printers use impact, but others are *thermal* in principal. They use special paper, and the print-head is heated. *Ink-jet printers* put the dot patterns on the paper by using very fine jets of ink.

Line printers

These operate so quickly that a whole line appears to be printed at once, although strictly speaking this is not so. Sets of print-heads revolve rapidly on a cylinder or a chain, and hammers strike the selected characters. The principle can be used in matrix printing.

Fig. 6.10 Line printer

Input and output methods **69**

Electrostatic printers

These print whole pages, or lines, at one operation. Special paper is used, on which electrical charges are placed in matrix fashion. The paper is brought into contact with powdered ink, and the print image is fixed to the paper by heat.

Laser printers

These also are page printers. The print image is first put on to the surface of a light-sensitive drum through a system of mirrors using low-power laser

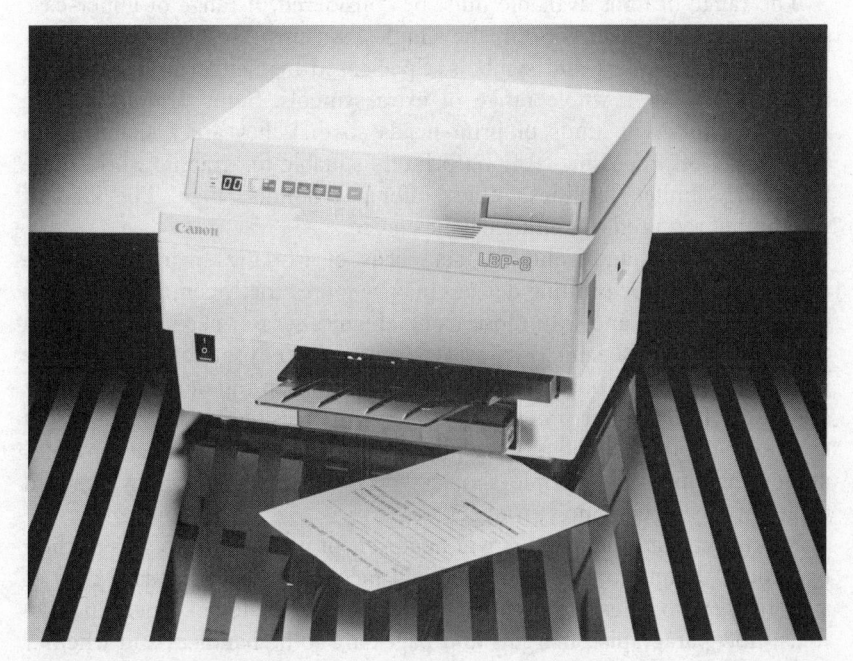

Fig. 6.11 Laser printer

beams. The activated parts of the surface attract ink particles, and the print is made permanent by heat or pressure.

Choice of printer

Not all the above printers are equally suitable for all computing work. A number of points need to be considered when buying a printer for a computer, or a computer with one.

Page printers will be much more expensive than other forms and will need a great volume of data processing to make them economically justifiable. The cheapest printers are those found in small hand-held calculators or provided as optional extras for home computers and other cheap computers.

The urgency with which data is needed, and the demand on computer time in output, are important factors. Generally, slower methods are less costly. A main-frame computer working to a three-shift system may need to print its output with much greater speed than a computer which a small business uses for a few hours each week. The quality of output required is a determining factor. Matrix printing is likely to be less clear than other kinds. Different kinds of printer vary in quality of alignment, accuracy of spacing and other points of interest to the user.

The range of fonts available must be considered. A range of upper-case letters will be adequate for only the simplest systems. Most will need lower-case letters, numbers and symbols. Specialised mathematical or scientific data will call for a whole range of extra symbols. Some printers can be used with different kinds of print-heads so that they are available for a wide range of processing. Among printers suitable for graphic work, some have fairly limited facilities, others offer a generous range. The kind of data output required will influence the choice.

Both statutory and voluntary standards of working environments are rising, and in future printing devices may be more strictly controlled. Impact printers are noisy, and with those using chemicals, laser beams or radiation the possibilities of health risks arise. Some printers produce only a single copy of the given output in one operation, others can run off large numbers of copies. Information processing is being increasingly used by firms of solicitors: they are unlikely to require mass printers, whereas a computer at the head office of a multiple-shop system may need to print a few hundred copies of each document it produces.

All but the simplest printers will need sets of instructions to govern their operations. Points to be determined will include whether standard rolls of stationery are to be used, or whether the paper is to be fed in concertina-like folds; how paragraphs, margins and pages are to be handled; and whether guillotines are to be brought into play. Choice of a particular kind of printer will take into account provision of such facilities, and the programs to operate them.

Computer output on microfiche (COM)

Readers buying a spare part from a large modern garage may have seen the storeman locate the item with the aid of a rectangular piece of film, which he places in an illuminating device and moves systematically about until a picture and description of the part appears on a screen. The piece of film is a *microfiche*, and it contains a part or whole of the spares catalogue, presented as a complete grid of pages arranged in rows and columns. The device magnifies the filmed record to a size convenient for reading. The required page is brought into view by co-ordinating vertical and horizontal controls. A similar system is used by some libraries to catalogue books and other material.

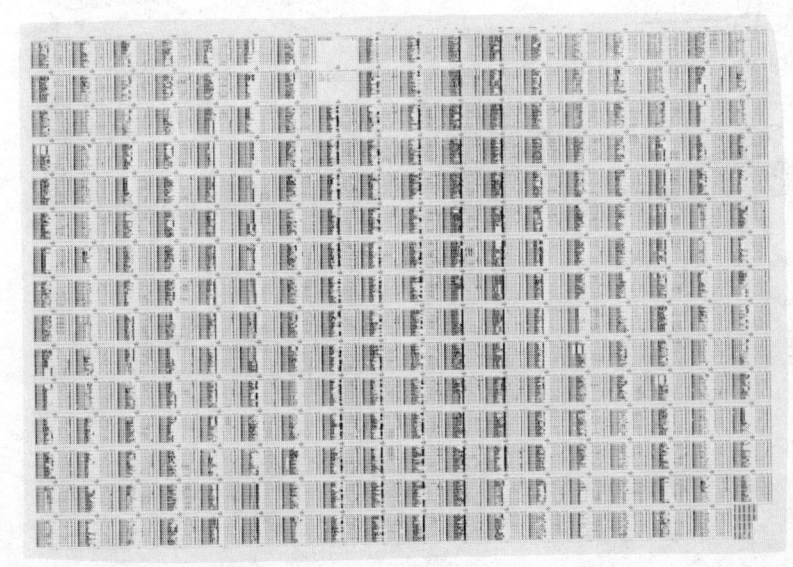

Fig. 6.12a   Microfiche

Computer output on microfiche media is 'computer output' because it is based on a photograph of a cathode-ray tube display, or obtained by transferring stored data using a laser beam or an electron beam. To a user new to the system, locating a particular page from 200, say, on one microfiche presents a problem, so that captions and codes may be provided on the final sheet to facilitate location. An alternative to microfiche is *microfilm* where the material is in a long roll, with a single – or double – line of pages.

Speech output

Devices emitting sound can be operated as computer output, electronic impulses being transformed to audible waves. The process of combining sound outputs to simulate human speech is known as speech synthesis. A pattern is obtained from computer recordings of the word to be output. The process is complicated, since detailed program instructions are needed

Information Management with Microfilm Fiche System

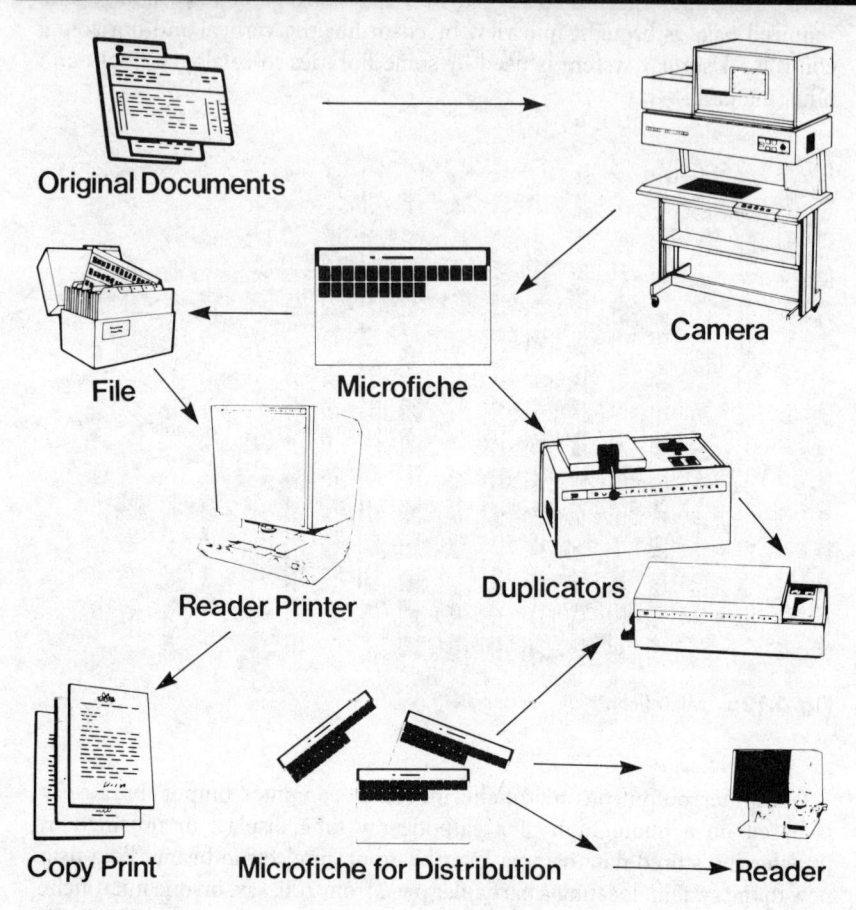

Fig. 6.12b Flow chart for microfiche procedure (*by courtesy of 3M United Kingdom PLC*)

to determine not only the wavelength of the sound but its amplitude, or loudness. Where such systems are used, the vocabulary is usually limited, but systems which allow complete words to be built up from basic recorded sounds allow greater latitude. *Audio response*, to use another name, has the advantage that the person receiving it is free to use his hands and eyes for other things. It can be used in the dark, and output is readily conveyed to blind people. A disadvantage is that output must not be slowed down, as the sense of individual words or a complete message is soon lost.

As techniques improve, the use of audio response is likely to increase. Machines are already available by which a travelling sales representative can place orders, and receive information about stock through the telephone of a customer he may be visiting. The same technique has been used for children's teaching machines.

Punched output

Punched cards and tape have been briefly mentioned already as storage and input media with the data being punched in by keyboard-operated machines. At one time output was recorded on punched cards and tapes. Even when cards and tape were widely used, the method was slow. These media are rapidly giving way to others, but in older systems output-punching machines may still be found.

Short questions

1   Briefly compare punched cards and magnetic tapes as input media under the following headings:
 (a) possibility of reuse;
 (b) method of input;
 (c) whether affected by outside magnetic fields;
 (d) effect of wear and tear.

2   A cheque and a meter-reading document both contain data which a computer can read. Distinguish between the ways in which data from each is read, and explain briefly the difference.

3   A supermarket's sales records are computerised and the bar codes on items bought are read at the check-out tills.
 (a) Explain why the bar codes do not state the prices of the items.
 (b) Explain how prices could be conveniently applied in making out the customer's bill.
 (c) Suggest two pieces of useful information the supermarket can obtain from all its check-out computer records from one store.

4   Explain in your own words what digitising techniques are. Give examples of (a) a business office, (b) a professional office where they may be used, indicating briefly the purposes for which they would be used.

5   (a) What problems would be encountered in voice impact of each of the following statements:
  (i) 'The student said the lecturer was out of his mind.'
  (ii) 'What this house needs is a little sun and air.'
 (b) Suggest how these and similar problems might be overcome.

6   In what input devices would you expect 'buffering', defined in Chapter 5, to be used, and why?

7   (a) What advantages does the displaying of computer output on a VDU offer to a businessman, when compared with other methods?
 (b) If a VDU is the only output, what disadvantages does he suffer?

8 Supposing a computer printer, unless otherwise instructed, will cover a page of output with printed lines from edge to edge and with no spaces between the characters (all of which would appear in lower case). Taking p. 70 of this book as an example, list all the kinds of extra instructions which which would need to be given if the material were to appear as in the book.

9 Suggest how a VDU could be used by each of the following:
 (a) a theatre booking office;
 (b) the branch office of an insurance company;
 (c) the head office of a political party.

10 A firm is buying its first computer, to be used for routine business processing and a limited amount of management information. Draft important questions which you would put to discover its needs. Underline technical terms in your questions, and below give brief explanatory notes of those terms.

Practical work

1 Collect as many examples of computer printing as practicable, including not only sheets of output on special stationery with special lining, but documents such as check-out bills and others with headings, etc., in ordinary printing and data added by computer processing. Examples could include data sheets used internally by small firms, employees' pay-chits, council rate demands, telephone bills and so on. Make brief notes about each example collected, giving examples of upper-case letters, lower-case letters, numbers and symbols. If possible try to discover where, how and when the computer printing occurred. Include your own comments on whether the printing was clear and whether the meaning of the data was clear to a lay person.

2 (a) Note by name all the input and output devices mentioned in this chapter.
 (b) Go through notes made in practical work in Chapters 1–5 (inclusive) and in assignment 1 above. State where input and output devices are used and, if possible, obtain permission to watch them at work, noting the source of incoming data and the destination of the output.
 (c) Where you have not found such devices, try to discover through libraries, the computing trade or otherwise where, outside your district, they can be obtained.
 (d) Use your findings to illustrate points made in this chapter.

Questions relevent to BTEC written examinations

1 (a) Give an account of different methods of input to computers using magnetic media, giving a different example for each method.
 (b) What factors are likely to determine in practice the choice of a particular method in preference to another?

Input and output methods **75**

2 (a) Describe devices for computer output, other than printers, and explain briefly how each method is used.

(b) Describe why such extensive use is made of the systems described in (a).

Other examination questions

1 Describe the various devices which are available for the input ot information to computing equipment. (IAM certificate – Methods and Systems paper, Winter 1985)

2 Describe the factors to be considered in deciding whether a particular application would best be served by a line printer, a matrix printer or a daisy-wheel printer. (IMS – Information Systems I, June 1984)

7 PROCESSING ROUTINES

> This chapter
> - describes how data is collected, validated and verified;
> - describes various processing methods, including on-line · real time · unit · batch · multiprocessing, and multiprogramming;
> - explains computer files, their creation · different kinds (including master, transaction), and relationships between generations;
> - describes file operations, including sorting · merging and searching.

Processing routines

Earlier chapters have described data and information processing and, in a general way, the parts played by the computer and supporting devices in these operations. This chapter will examine in more detail a variety of paths which an initial input of data follows until it leaves the computer system as output.

Data collection

A common method of entry to the processing system is through transfer of data from a *source document,* i.e. a document originating outside the system on which it is written. A worker's hours, for example, will be read from his weekly time-sheet by a keyboard operator and hence input on to a magnetic disk or tape. A candidate's answers to a multi-choice question is another example, the document being read by a special input device at the examining board's data centre. The term *data capture* is sometimes used synonymously with data collection, but some writers restrict it to describing direct entry through a machine, as occurs at computerised cash-tills or library desks, where no document circulates independently before transfer.

Data validation

Extra precautions are needed in processing data by computer. A system will slavishly follow every instruction it is given, but a computer has no inherent common sense to detect and remove obvious errors, unless especially instructed. A government clerk would know, for example, that a claim for maternity benefit was false if a document gave the woman's age as 95, but a computer would accept the data unless a suitable test had been imposed. A *validation* procedures program checks to ensure that the data is acceptable for processing.

A *limit check* which rejected ages outside child-bearing limits would have rejected 95, and prevented the computer's error. In a similar way, a check which rejected negative marks or any greater than 100 could be introduced in a program processing examination marks where the accepted range was 0–100. Validation checks can also test whether data is in the required format. For instance, a house number should not be in letters, and a surname should not be in numbers. The size of a record can be checked: except in historical records, a year of birth should always occupy four spaces before coding. Checks can ascertain whether an item of data is present, such as the registration number of a vehicle where an insurance company is processing an accident claim.

Other checks

When data in bit form is transferred during processing, there is some risk of a bit at the end of a byte being lost so that, for example, a line of 15 bits instead of 16 enters the next stage. A *parity check* guards against this. Where, as in this case, the group is of even-number size, a '1' is added making it odd. The computer tests the group size, and if it is even, then the data is rejected. Another parity-check system extends the group to an even number of bits, and tests the data accordingly.

A *check digit* system can reduce errors in processing large numbers such as account numbers. The number to be protected is given an extra place by putting a digit to the extreme right so that the new number is exactly divisible by a stated modulus, 11 being a common figure. The computer tests all the new numbers, rejecting any that are not divisible by 11 as erroneous. For example:

A customer's account number is 64123.
$64123 \div 11 = 5829 + 4R$.
The remainder, 4, is the check digit and is placed to the extreme right of the original account number to give an artificial number for processing purposes.

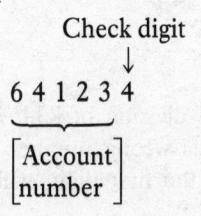

$$\begin{array}{c} \text{Check digit} \\ \downarrow \\ 6\ 4\ 1\ 2\ 3\ 4 \\ \underbrace{\qquad\qquad}_{\begin{bmatrix}\text{Account}\\ \text{number}\end{bmatrix}} \end{array}$$

Where the remainder in calculating the check digit is 10, the check digit is $(11 - 10) = 1$, and it is *added* to the data, not placed at the end, as illustrated below.

An item of vehicle data is a mileage of 42,943,

$$11 \overline{)42,943} \\ 3,903 + 10R$$

giving a check digit of $(11 - 10) = 1$, the augmented data being printed as

/4/2/9/4/3//01

showing that the 1 must be added in:

$$42,943 \\ \underline{+1} \\ 11\overline{)42,944} \\ 3,904 + 0R$$

A correct version of the original data would therefore be accepted.

Other moduli are used in the calculation of check digits, and for them the procedure just followed must always be used. In sales data, an item of 890 units is prepared for use with a modulus of 17:

$$890 \div 17 = 52 + 6R.$$

Therefore the check digit is $(17-6) = 11$, and the data is written

8/9/0//11.

Checking,

$$890 \\ \underline{+11} \\ 17\overline{)901} \\ 53 + 0R$$

so the data would be accepted.

That the method is not always effective is shown by finding a check digit for 8345. Division by 11 gives

$$758 + 7R$$

so that it would appear

8/3/4/5/7.

If in processing the number appears as 8346, then division of 83467 by 11 will produce a remainder that is not 0, and this wrong number will be rejected. In the same way 93457, a mistake in the first digit, will be rejected. Suppose, however, the digits 8 and 4 in the original number were interchanged, the computer would not reject the wrong number, 43857, because division by 11 produces a remainder of 0.

A more elaborate system, using weights, reduces greatly the risk of errors being missed. Digits are weighted increasingly, from units through tens and hundreds to thousands, etc. Using the data 8345 used in the last calculation, weights of 5, 4, 3 and 2 are applied to the respective digits. The sum of the products is divided by 11, the remainder is noted, and subtracting it from 11 gives the required check digit. To check, the computer reverses the steps in the calculations, weighting the check digit by 1. If the sum of the new products is divisible by 11 without remainder, the data is accepted. Three calculations illustrate the method.

(a) Calculating the check digit for 8345

Digit	Weight	Product
8	5	40
3	4	12
4	3	12
5	2	10
		74

$74 \div 11 = 6 + 8R.$

Therefore check digit $= 11 - 8 = 3.$

(b) Computer processing of correct data with check digit

Digit	Weight	Product
8	5	40
3	4	12
4	3	12
5	2	10
3	1	3
		77

$77 \div 11 = 7 + 0R.$

Therefore computer would accept the data.

(c) Application to 43853, which computer under first system accepted

The extended number would be 43853.

Digit	Weight	Product
4	5	20
3	4	12
8	3	24
5	2	10
3	1	3
		69

$69 \div 11 = 6 + 3R$.

Remainder is not 0, and the data would be rejected.

Although check digits may be generated by computers, this may be expensive. Other alternatives to manual calculation are the use of special machines and the use of special tables setting out pages of code numbers and suitable check digits.

Verification

In early days of computing, much data entered computers through punched tape and punched cards, with greater scope for human error than is afforded by more modern methods. Most systems therefore made careful provision for verification, i.e. checking the punching to ensure that the original records had been accurately transferred. The general method was to have a second record prepared by another operator, and to compare mechanically or otherwise the two versions. An adaptation of the system enables verification of the contents of a magnetic disk or tape. One system allows the second operator to key in the data afresh and compare it with data run back from the first disk. Comparison may be made with the help of a VDU. Upon completion the data, corrected if need be, is run back on to a disk. Earlier validation may have reduced the task of verification.

The computer and its links

In the simplest computing system, data input is physically brought to the computer and processed by it, and the output is physically taken away from it. Such an arrangement would be adequate for a small system, and the next chapter will describe how large systems may use computer bureau services to convey data in this way. Generally, however, most computers will receive input through a separate device, at a small or great distance, connected by a circuit. An example would be a keyboard and VDU at a branch of a commercial bank through which data could be fed into the bank's main-frame computer at head office. Such a device is an example of a *terminal* and it is said to be *on-line* with other computers. These terms are also applicable to output devices, for example a VDU in a stockbroker's office which displays the latest share prices or currency exchange rates. Most, but not all, on-line arrangements are speedy enough to enable data to be produced for an on-the-spot decision to be made on a point in question or immediate action to be taken. An enquiry from a travel agent's branch about passenger vacancies on an airline flight is one example; another is in a computer-based library where an assistant at the desk can ascertain almost immediately whether a borrower has reached the maximum number of volumes allowed by the lending regulation. Such operations are called *real-time*.

Batch processing

In the early days of computing, commercial applications became attractive when it was realised that a computer had the capacity to perform large numbers of relatively simple operations quickly and cheaply, such as producing pay-roll slips each week or making out customers' bills towards the end of each month. The most effective way of doing this was to collect all the documents of a similar kind and process them in one run over a short period of time, or perhaps with the oldest punched-media systems, two or three times. The operation, still extensively used, is called *batch processing*.

A number of controls must be used if batching is to be effective. The aim is to prevent error by loss or misplacement of data by non-inclusion or loss of documents. Once received, the total input of documents is organised into manageable batches. These may be of equal size, e.g. sets of 100 workers' time-sheets, or the size of each batch may relate to a working unit, e.g. the billing of a month's sales of goods may be batched for each of 20 working days of the month, with variations in batch size. Documents received, and documents put-out, which will include output data, are logged in a register and signatures obtained. Each batch will have a unique reference number, and this, with other information such as the number of items in the batch, will appear on the *batch cover-note*. Another check depends upon *hash totals*. These are the totals of an individual number, such as an employee's works number or an examination candidate's entrance number, which appears on every item in a batch. The hash total for a whole run will be the total of the sub-totals appearing on each batch cover note, and each sub-total will be the total of all the work numbers or similar values in the batch. A computer program will count the number of documents, the number of batches and the intermediate and final hash totals. Discrepancies will soon be detected and errors located by the program or by manual analysis of documents and print-outs.

Batching has disadvantages. Whereas manual processing of time-sheets, bills and stock returns can be reasonably spread over a working period, so that staff employment is even, batching involves peaking of human effort and computer time unless other suitable work can be found for what would otherwise be slack time. Furthermore, as batches build up, documents are out of reach until processing is completed. Although a number of controls can be imposed, accidental inclusion of rogue data or documents, or a computing malfunction, may seriously upset the work-flow in a business or other organisation.

Multiprogramming

So far, processing has been described as a series of separate operations, one after the other, carried out by the input devices, other computers and then the output devices. Often, input and output devices perform more slowly than the computer, and the slowest device determines the speed of the complete processing cycle. This means that the CPU does not run continuously, but in fits and starts. Only one program can be run at one time by a single CPU. If, however, two or more programs are available and their operations can be synchronised, the gaps in operation can be reduced. For example, when the CPU would have to pause because output is still being transferred to an outside device, a second program can use the short break to read more data from a tape or disk. This is known as *multiprogramming*. A similar kind of economy can occur through *multiprocessing*, a system by which two or more CPUs having common peripherals can maintain a common processing operation by running simultaneously two or more programs, with a convenient allocation of the separate stages between them.

Other processing modes

In *transaction processing*, the computer operates as soon as processing is needed, and there is no queueing as there is with batch processing. The input often starts several programs. For example, when a university registers a new student by computer, data would enter not only the registry but the faculty records, the library, the accommodation department and perhaps be transmitted automatically to the students' union office.

In a *time-sharing system*, a computer is linked to two or more users, each with a terminal. The computer itself will operate continuously, being available to each terminal in turn for a very short period of time, with this cycle of input returning again and again. The unit of availability is called a *time-slice*. This short span may allow the input of a great deal of data which, if need be, can be stored and returned at a later time. Batch processing can be used with a time-sharing system. It is especially useful where processing takes time because of involved calculations or extensive searches for data.

Storage and processing units

Three units have been mentioned so far, the *bit*, a binary digit (either 0 or 1), a *byte* (usually of eight bits to represent a character) and a *word*, which is a set of bits, the smallest unit handled by a computer in a single processing operation. A *record* is a meaningful arrangement of data, such as

> A. E. Ferguson, 3 High Road, Moortown (1974)

taken from a computerised list of members of the Home Gardens Club; the bracketed year is the date when he joined. It would, of course, be held in binary code. Another example of a record is

> NX29 – 6 cm × 10 cm brackets, steel, drilled – (12 doz.)

from a stock-list of engineering spares, 12 dozen being the present stock level. Each record is composed of parts which individually are meaningful, e.g. Ferguson's address, and the code for the brackets. On the storage medium (e.g. disk) each part occupies part or whole of a defined width, called a *field*. The term was used originally to describe vertical space allocations on punched cards. In designing a system of records and fields, allowance must be made for the maximum length likely to be needed. In the first example above, the town might be 'Tadchester-on-the-Wolds', and in the second a component might be '15 cm × 30 cm × 120 cm, corner-piece, gun-metal'. An organised set of records is stored on a file, discussed on p. 84.

The commonest storage media for files today are magnetic disks, tapes or drums. One set of records, e.g. an electricity board's list of all its customers, may occupy more than one file.

Arranging data within files

Data is put on to magnetic tape in blocks, and within blocks in fields. Gaps separate the fields and the blocks to allow deceleration of the moving tape to enable reading of data and acceleration when reading is complete. Records may be placed on file *serially*, i.e. in the order in which they occur: for example a firm would record one order on file, and the next order would go on next, and so on. In *sequential* filing, records are made in a predetermined, relevant order, e.g. a payroll would be alphabetically arranged and where a firm had a large number of customers distributed throughout the country, records might be arranged in geographically defined sales areas.

Each tape will start with a computer-readable label, stating the contents, a serial number where a set of records uses more than one tape and in some cases its generation status, a term explained later in this chapter. The label is likely to refer to the programs used with it, and where its contents are temporary, the date before which they may not be overwritten. A final label may repeat classification data on the first label and state the number of blocks on the tape. Each field is identified by a *key*, a statement in code to enable it to be located and processed.

Data on a disk is held in narrow circular bands, divided into sectors by interblock gaps, along the outer parts of the radii. In a fixed-disk scheme, each surface, track and block is numbered so that the read/write-head can locate a particular record using an address system. For convenient access to data, a number of blocks are organised into a unit of storage called a *bucket*. In a stack of disks when the read/write-arms are in use, in any given position, the tracks they will be serving will have equal radii and will coincide in outline with an imaginary cylinder. Related data, therefore, can be stored in the same relative position on each disk and access can be obtained from one position of the set of read/write-heads. This arrangement is the *cylinder* method.

Files and data movement

Computer files, as mentioned earlier, serve the same general purposes as the office files they replaced, but the whole system must be more rigorously organised. A firm buying goods, selling goods on credit and using a system of monthly invoices would need a number of files in order to take full advantage of computerisation. Data for printing out invoices would be held on a computer file, and the file would be kept for some time in case of disputes, debt collection or analysis for management reports. It would be an example of a *master file*, i.e. a major one, which is not purely temporary. Other files of this kind which enjoy a fairly permanent existence hold the customers' accounts with the firm, and a record of stock held.

Processing an invoice file will involve printing customers' names and addresses. They are likely to be held on a separate file, which would be used in a postal advertising campaign, or for organising representatives' calls. This is an example of an *information or reference file*.

All files will need to be kept up to date; in a computerised system incoming information will be entered into temporary files, and from time to time it will be transferred through the computer to the appropriate master file. For example, when new stock enters, or existing stock is sold or written-off, the events will be recorded on a special file, probably called a *stock movement file*. This is a *transaction file*. Transfer of data from this file to the stock file at regular intervals will ensure the actual and recorded stock levels agree. The Personnel Department of a large undertaking will keep a record of employees on a personnel file. This will be updated from a *movement file*, another name for a transaction file, in which changes due to new appointments, dismissals, resignations, etc., have been recorded.

Generations of files

Special care is needed in computer file operations as computer records are more easily destroyed or mislaid than records in older filing systems. Many organisations maintain for security purposes a cyclical system by which at any one time three successive editions are available. A simple illustration (Table 7.1) shows the organisation of a master file, or stock file. On 21

Table 7.1

File 'generation'	Date	Changes in level during week (units)		Level at date
		In	Out	
A	7 Feb.			237
		13	50	
B	14 Feb.			200
		51	43	
C	21 Feb.			208

February, versions A, B and C would be in existence. They would be distinguished as 'grandfather' (A), 'father' (B) and 'son' (C). On 28 February, data would be erased from the old grandfather file (A) and a new level, calculated by applying the most recent 'in' and 'out' figures to the last stock figure of 208, would be entered on to the cleared file. The original grandfather file would die, and the others would be a generation older, as shown in Table 7.2.

Table 7.2

Code	21 February	28 February
A	Grandfather	Dead 28 February
B	Father	Grandfather
C	Son	Father
A_1*	–	Son

* On storage media used for A.

Supposing, on 21 February, the 'son' stock file was accidentally erased, then the record could be restored by re-running the 'father' version with the stock movement file. In practice, stock changes would be likely to affect a whole range of products, but the generation system just explained could still be applied.

Sorting

Items of data may be placed on a file in the order in which they occur, but re-arranging the items in a systematic order has advantages. It will help location of particular items, make print-outs of the file easier to understand and use, be an advantage for some forms of business operation such as credit control, and facilitate the merging of files. Sometimes the items are sorted into alphabetical order (e.g. lists of customers by surname), sometimes by descending order of size (as with examination marks), and sometimes with the lowest number first (house numbers in a street directory). One method is to have predetermined positions in alphabetical or numerical sequence on a disk or tape and run the file on to it, but this may leave gaps.

A *bubble sort* uses a computer's ability to compare two numbers and choose the greater. A very simple example of sorting examination results (Table 7.3) into order of merit illustrates the method. Each stage of the operation is called a 'pass', a term originally used to describe sets of punched cards going through a sorting machine. Starting from the left, the first pair of numbers is compared (A and B) and interchanged if the larger one is on the right; C and D are similarly treated, and then E and F. The second pass in this example starts with B and C being compared. Passes continue until all the marks are in the required order; in this case only three passes are needed. The capital letters A–F simply define the positions, and are not part of the data.

Table 7.3
Examination marks: Haines 36, Brown 95, George 00, Smith 81, Edwin 50, Yates 19.

	A	B	C	D	E	F
Original position	36	95	00	81	50	19
After 1st pass	95	36	81	00	50	19
After 2nd pass	95	81	36	50	00	19
After 3rd pass	95	81	50	36	19	00

Merging

Supposing a firm kept a file for each of two shifts of workers, the files could be arranged in this fashion:

Shift I	*Shift II*
Jackson	Griffiths (B)
Old	Nicholson
Adams	Yates
Wiggins	Bennet
Fellows	Griffiths (A)
Baker	Roberts
Thompson	
Knight	

Reorganisation of the work-force combines both shifts into one new one, and the file is now in alphabetical order. It would look like this:

New shift
Adams
Baker
Bennet
Fellows
Griffiths (A)
Griffiths (B)
Jackson
Knight
Nicholson
Old
Roberts
Thompson
Wiggins
Yates

Merging is simply putting the contents of two corresponding files together. In this example, the processing would have been quicker and simpler if the original shift files had been alphabetically ordered.

Searching for data

If items of data on a file are not arranged in sequence, locating a particular item is likely to be a long process, as every item starting from the beginning must be tested until the one required is found. In the long run, the average number of items per file to be tested would be half the total for the file. If items are arranged in numerical order, the *binary search* method is likely to prove quicker. Assuming that the file is full, the contents are divided into halves: one will clearly not contain the required item so the other is chosen. The process is repeated with this half, sub-division on this rule continuing until the required item is found or its absence demonstrated. A simplified example of the principle follows.

Eight works numbers are stored sequentially in eight consecutive locations, and no. 819 is required.

Location	No.	
1	003	
2	195	reject (1)
3	468	
4	532	

⟶ First split

| 5 | 667 | reject (2) |
| 6 | 712 | |

⟶ Second split

| 7 | 819} *Required number* | |

⟶ Third split

| 8 | 921} reject (3) | |

Briefly, the steps are:

(*a*) The first split is between locations 4 and 5;
819 > 532, therefore the numerically upper half is taken.
(*b*) The second split is between locations 6 and 7;
819 > 712, therefore the numerically upper half is taken.
(*c*) The third split is between locations 7 and 8,
and 819 is identified as the sole number of the upper half.

This operation may simply occur because 819 has left the firm and his record needs to be removed. More probably, locating it is the first step in further processing, e.g. regrading the worker or discovering his length of service. In practice, the file would contain other data such as names and addresses and weekly rates of pay. This example has been simplified in order to explain binary search.

Databases and databanks

An organisation which computerised its records might soon find that it produced a large and growing number of files, e.g. some for invoices, some for sales, some for customers' accounts, some for stock-holding. Analysis would soon reveal that the same item appeared on two or more files, for instance a customer's name on the account file, on an invoice file and on a file recording the despatch of stock. An alternative system would be to store all the data centrally on a system designed to meet present use of data and to anticipate future development. Such a store would be available to all data users in the organisation, and would be called a *database*.

An obvious advantage of such an arrangement would be economy in storage. Much of the original data would be *redundant*, and in many situations the single recording of a particular item, such as an employee's name, would be all that was required. However, in some systems, more than one record of the same item would be kept, under a system of *planned redundancy*. A further advantage would be economy in updating records, and a lessening of the risk that mutually inconsistent records of the same item of data could exist at the same time. An even greater advantage today is that with centralised data it is easier to meet the dangers explained in Chapter 16, lack of security, removal of privacy and contravention of data protection legislation.

The setting up and running of a database requires special software, and often a *database management system* will be provided. A *database manager* and staff will be responsible for the input of data, processing, security and output.

A larger unit of storage is the *databank*. Precise definition of this aggregate is less easy, but it is usually taken to mean two or more databases under one control. A government department, for example, could hold in one base data relating to its entire staff, and in another data relating to thousands of members of the public whom it directly served.

Short questions

1 Give an example of a different source document which you would expect to be used by each of the following organisations, explaining why the document would be useful:
   (a) a national newspaper;
   (b) a national school examination body;
   (c) a builders' merchant.

2 List the various checks applied to input data, stating briefly for each the kind of error it is intended to prevent.

3 Write down your year of birth. Calculate a check digit using modulus 11 and explain how the check would be used.

4 Provide 9199 with a check digit using modulus 17, showing what would happen if in processing the first two digits of the new numbers were reversed. Repeat the operation, using weights.

5 Explain briefly the advantages which (a) multiprogramming and (b) multiprocessing can separately bring to computer systems. What is needed if both techniques are to be applied to any system?

6 A civil engineering firm constructs roads, bridges and other public works throughout the UK. It has a full-time staff of engineers and other professional and technical people and a key work-force of its own tradesmen. At any

one time, it operates on a number of different sites, employing at each large numbers of temporary and mainly unskilled workers. It makes extensive use of computers in processing business records.

(a) Give two examples of batch processing which it could use.

(b) Give one example of transaction processing.

Give reasons for your choice.

7 One of the following statements is correct, one incorrect. Select the correct one and explain, with a suitable illustration, why the other is incorrect:

(a) Processing on-line must be in real-time.

(b) Processing in real-time must be on-line.

8 Using terms explained in this chapter, how would you classify each of the following files, and why?

(a) An estate agent's file of all the properties he has for sale.

(b) A computer manufacturer's file giving particulars of a number of transport firms he can hire for collecting raw materials and distributing his products.

(c) A file used by a fan club to record annual subscriptions as they are paid by members.

9 Extend the numerical data given in the account of file generations by adding the following transactions:

25 February: received 15 units, none went out.

6 March: received 15 units, 23 units were issued.

Update the records, giving the dates, generations and stock levels of the three latest files.

10 A large transport organisation has a master file giving details of every vehicle it owns. Give two consecutive entries as they would appear on a print-out, indicating at least three different fields used in the file.

11 Number all the letters of the alphabet, thus A (1), B (2), ..., Z (26). Apply the numbers to the first letters of the candidates' names on p. 86, e.g. had there been a 'Donaldson, 49' it would read (4) Donaldson '49. Repeat the sorting exercise, but using the alphabetical numbers as the basis.

12 Two large independent supermarket firms with computerised records have a number of branches each. They amalgamate.

(a) Give examples of files at the new head office which would need to be merged, giving a brief account of the use which would be made of the new files.

(b) Mention difficulties you would expect to encounter in the file-merging operations.

13 In an industrial experiment, the times taken by ten different workers to perform the same task were as follows:

Worker's code	Time
1	3 min 00 s
2	2 min 47 s

Processing routines

3	2 min 48 s
4	4 min 15 s
5	3 min 33 s
6	3 min 30 s
7	3 min 03 s
8	2 min 46 s
9	4 min 14 s
10	2 min 13 s

(a) Show the operation of the *first pass only* to sort the list with the quickest worker first and the slowest last.

(b) Set out the list as it would appear on the file when sorting had been completed.

(c) Follow the general method shown on pp. 87 and 88 which would enable you to find the worker with a time of 4 min 14 s. (*Note:* Particular division may produce unequally sized sub-groups, but the method still works.)

(d) Suppose you had been asked to search for a worker with a time of 2 min 50 s. What would you expect to happen?

Practical work

1 Collect as many examples of documents as possible relating to as many businesses, government departments, local councils, clubs and other organisations as possible. Whether or not they are used in computerised systems, suppose that they are.

State for each:
   (a) examples of data that could be obtained (some forms may yield different kinds of data);
   (b) examples of computer file(s) on to which the data could pass;
   (c) the purpose of processing the data;
   (d) occasions when the contents of files would be sorted.

2 Study the use of conventional, non-computerised files in a firm or organisation which is not computerised, or only partly computerised. For each kind of file, state:
   (a) general nature of contents;
   (b) source of input;
   (c) any output;
   (d) changes in that file which computerisation would bring.

Questions relevant to BTEC written examinations

1 Outline the methods for carrying out the following processes, and explain why each method is used:
   (a) batch processing;
   (b) multiprocessing;
   (c) multiprogramming.

2 (a) Explain what a computer file is.
(b) Distinguish between a *master file* and a *transaction file*, illustrating how each could be used in the same business system.
(c) What is the purpose of each of the following file operations:
(i) sorting;
(ii) merging;
(iii) searching?

Other examination questions

1   A company operates its data-processing system on the batch-processing method.
You are required to state the stages involved in producing a transaction file, giving a brief description of the tasks involved at each stage. Your answer should indicate the purpose of the 'batch control slip', and suggest its possible content. Present your answers in a tabulated form,
   i.e. (a) ....
       (b) ....
(AAT – Data Processing, June 1983)

2   (a) Define and describe an example of each of the following:
(i) Master File;
(ii) Transaction File;
(iii) Reference file.
(b) What are the factors that need to be considered when designing a master file?
(c) What are the major considerations governing the choice of hardware used for the storage of a file?
(IDPM – Systems Analysis and Design 1, June 1985)

3   Your organisation's computer steering committee has decided to introduce a database administration system.
(a) Describe how a database differs from traditional computer files.
(b) Discuss the factors which could have persuaded the committee to make this change. (IAM – Summer 1984)

8 MAIN-FRAME AND OTHER COMPUTERS

This chapter

- describes the capabilities and work of main-frame computers, microprocessors and minicomputers;
- distinguishes between digital and analogue computers;
- summarises criteria for choosing a computer.

The capabilities and work of main-frame computers

The main-frame computer still retains an important position in data and information processing despite competition from a variety of smaller and very useful modern machines. These are adaptable and meet a whole range of needs, but cannot match the main-frame in storage capacity, work-load and speed of processing.

The main-frame can serve many more terminals than any of its rivals and certain peripherals, e.g. the largest up-to-date printing devices, that are impossible with smaller computers can be used with it. Another advantage is that a main-frame will be able to work with programs in a greater range of languages than a smaller computer. The computer itself will be expensive to purchase, and it will be built on a permanent foundation. An air-conditioning system will need to be provided and maintained, because of susceptibility to dust, humidity and fluctuations in temperature. Whereas the simplest types of computer can be used by primary school children, a main-frame computer will need the full-time services of trained personnel paid at professional rates.

Microprocessors

The development of smaller computers owes much to the coming of *microprocessors*. By a striking advance in miniaturisation technology, a complete CPU can be implanted on the surface of a silicon chip. The manufacture of microprocessors depends upon the chemical fixing of photographed circuits. No assembly or separate connections are needed, and mass production keeps costs low. Microprocessors are used in their own right in computing systems.

The input from a number of terminals linked to a main-frame computer needs controlling and synchronising. For these tasks, special microprocessors known as *front-end processors* are used.

Microcomputers

The addition of an internal memory and input and output circuits to a microprocessor gives it the ability of a complete computer. This can be done by adding one or more chips, keeping the miniature scale, and a *microcomputer* is the result. Most microcomputers used in business are portable

Fig. 8.1 Microcomputer

and can be plugged into an ordinary power point. They are used with floppy disks. A VDU may be an integral part of the computer, or it may be an optional extra, or (with a simple adaptor) a TV screen may be used instead. A simple printer may be provided. Data is usually entered, and the computer controlled, through a keyboard. Some microcomputers are smaller than normal typewriters. The largest would occupy the top of the average office desk. The commonest business applications are invoicing, ledger work, payroll processing and operations based on data stores, such as running off lists of customers, or doing work formerly undertaken by addressographs.

Another form, the *personal* or *home computer*, has become very popular. With them, address books can be computerised, personal accounts kept, cooking recipes stored and computer games played. Another field of development is the use of microprocessors in teaching data processing and computing science, and in aided learning in other subjects.

In most of these applications, the microcomputer will operate as an isolated unit. They are being used, however, very extensively in distributed systems, in which they are linked to main-frame computers, as mentioned in Chapter 3.

Most microcomputers will be built with two storage systems. The first will be ROM, controlling the internal operation of the microprocessor, and handling the outside programming instructions. An ROM will be initially programmed by the manufacturer and the user will not be able to alter this program. Where the microcomputer has a PROM (programmable ROM) instead, the user can program it, but he must be accurate, since a programming error is difficult to rectify. Storage with EPROM ('E' standing for erasable) is better since the program can be altered by ultraviolet light. An even more convenient version is EAROM, where the program is electronically alterable.

The second storage system, RAM (random access memory), will contain the application program, i.e. the program applying a particular technique such as invoicing to the data, which can also be stored in RAM.

The microcomputers mentioned so far are manufactured in large numbers, to fairly standard designs with the needs of broad classes of users in mind. Microcomputers employing numbers of chips assembled on boards can be made to meet particular needs, or supplied in kit form to amateur enthusiasts for assembly. They are called *board-line machines*. One established use is for staff training in computing technique.

Minicomputers

Standing in price, capacity and power between main-frame computers and microcomputers are minicomputers. They resemble main-frame computers, but are smaller and more robust, for the working environment need not be conditioned. They offer multiprogramming economies and can stand at the centre of a small distributed system; these are advantages they have over microcomputers. In some fields, larger microcomputers offer strong competition with small minicomputers.

Digital and analog computers

Computers discussed so far in this book have been *digital*. This means that data has been input in the form of bits, and after processing the output has been in the form of digits. Readers finding the time with a digital watch

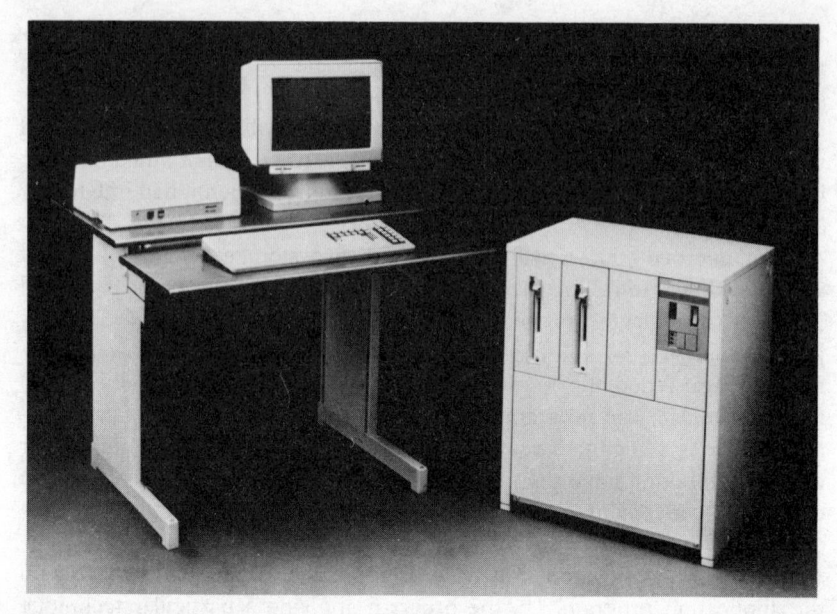

Fig. 8.2 Minicomputer

will know that the dial can only state it in whole numbers; successive intervals of time follow in series of jerks, e.g. 6 h 59 min 58 s/6 h 59 min 59 s/7 h 0 min 0 s. The mechanism gives no opportunity for estimating time in intermediate intervals, such as $59\frac{1}{2}$ s. The moving hands of the older type of watch traverse evenly through a given unit of time and would allow fine intervals of measurement. Some computers work with measurements that can be made all along the scale, responding to changes in voltage, length or temperature for example. Such computers are *analog*. They are mainly used in scientific and industrial control applications, e.g. monitoring the acidity of chemical solutions. They have little direct application to modern data processing. Devices are available for converting digital values to analog, and analog to digital. Computers which can operate as both digital and analog machines are called *hybrid*.

Choosing a computer

A number of criteria, in addition to cost, which will guide choice of a particular type of computer have already emerged in the brief accounts given of particular machines, such as type of work, volume, convenience and speed. Where new devices are being added to old, *compatability* is important, i.e. the need for two devices to work technically together. Not all terminals, for example, are acceptable to all main-frame computers. The coming of

Main-frame and other computers **97**

word processors, machines which improve the capabilities and performance of the office typewriter by incorporating computing facilities, is a new factor. These newcomers are described more fully in Chapter 12. Differences in word length determine the speed and power of computers and affect programming techniques. A computer which can handle the longest word-length has a great advantage over others which cannot.

A firm or organisation needing computing facilities will not take into account merely installing its own systems. It will look to a whole range of services offered from outside, and the next chapter will describe these.

Short questions

1 Why will main-frame computers cost more to purchase, install and run than other types?

2 Explain the difference between a microprocessor and a microcomputer.

3 Some firms use only a main-frame computer, some use only microprocessors, and some use both. Explain this fact, illustrating your answer by giving examples of the work handled in the different situations.

4 If all the needs of computer users can be met by main-frame computers and microcomputers, why are minicomputers still being produced and used?

5 A firm buys goods and distributes them retail through its own ten shops. It has not been computerised before, but proposes buying a microcomputer.
   (*a*) Explain briefly three different tasks to which the computer could be applied.
   (*b*) Mention a few changes in the organisation and staffing of the firm which you would expect the coming of the microcomputer to bring.

6 A firm is to buy its first main-frame computer. Give a reasoned account of important costs it is likely to incur, besides the actual purchase.

Practical work

1 A local firm wishes to introduce computers into its business processes, but will not need a main-frame computer. By studying advertisements and contacting local agents and suppliers give general information under the following headings:
   (*a*) types of computer, and where obtainable;
   (*b*) capabilities, kind of processes undertaken;
   (*c*) software;
   (*d*) installation requirements, if any;
   (*e*) maintenance, servicing;
   (*f*) other points of interest.

2 You have been invited to contribute a few paragraphs to a magazine read by businessmen who do not necessarily have a technical knowledge of computing, under the title 'Small versus large computers'.

(a) Give paragraph headings.
(b) State what photographs or diagrams you would like to have to illustrate the article.
(c) Write out the first paragraph of not less than 250 words.

Questions relevant to BTEC written examination

1 (a) Distinguish between *main-frame computers*, *microcomputers*, and *minicomputers*.
(b) Why are all three types made and used today?

2 A business with manual clerical systems has decided to computerise them. Explain important factors to be considered in deciding the kinds and numbers of computers to be obtained.

Other examination questions

1 The Training Director of your company, which currently does not have its own computer system, is organising a seminar for its junior executives on the use of computers. You have been asked to participate in the instruction team and have been given several areas of the subject to prepare for explanation during the seminar.
Required: Prepare notes on *four* of the following topic areas so that they may be used in the seminar.
(a) What do we mean by a main-frame computer system?
(b) What do we mean by a microcomputer?
(c) What is the function of a word-processor system?
(d) Outline the staffing structure that would be required to run a main-frame computer system.
(e) Outline the principle of check-digit verification used during the data validation (sometimes known as data vet) stage of data processing.
(ACCA – Preliminary Examination, Numerical Analysis and Data Processing paper, Dec. 1983)

2 A small company is considering buying a microcomputer. They require professional advice as to a choice of machine out of the many now available. Explain how they should approach the problem and describe *ten* criteria they should consider. (IDPM – Data Processing Part II, Dec. 1985)

9 COMPUTER SERVICES

This chapter
- describes the work of computer bureaux and of other organisations supporting computer systems;
- explains points to be considered in service agreements;
- introduces the concepts of cost benefit, effectiveness and efficiency.

Computer service organisations

The account on computing given in this book so far has assumed that a firm or organisation needing to apply computer technology to its data and

```
CMG
IBM Authorised Dealer
INFORMATION CONSULTANCY & PROCESSING
 - Computer Consultancy
 - Analysis and Design
 - Programming
 - Bureau Processing
 - Hardware Suppliers
An extensive range of packages and
systems are used by over 6000 customers
BIRMINGHAM BRISTOL EDINBURGH GLASGOW GUILDFORD LONDON MANCHESTER
01-638 3791
```

```
Computer Mailing
Services Ltd
BUREAU SERVICES OFFERED:
On-line General Accounting
Subscription Accounting
Controlled Circulation
Reader Enquiry Service
Trade and Retail Distribution
Direct Product Marketing
List Creation/Deduplication
Automatic Rebate Coding
DOS/VSE Time Hire

28 Charing Cross Road
London WC2H 0AU
01-240 2307
```

Fig. 9.1 Advertisements for computer bureaux

information processing has made its own unaided arrangements, i.e. it has bought the computer and peripherals, engaged professional and technical staff and written its own software. This is true for many firms, but some use the services offered by specialist businesses from outside. The ranges of such services vary widely and firms differ very much in the extent to which they use them. The specialists are mainly known as *computer service bureaux*, although some services are offered by firms trading under a different name.

Turnkey system

A firm wishing to enjoy computer services with the maximum help from outside will enter into a contract for a *turnkey arrangement*. The computer, software and peripherals are provided as a complete system from outside. Sometimes the agreement will be made with a large manufacturer. Some systems are installed through the services of *computer consultants*. These are individual professional people who advise on various aspects of computing. Some bureaux offer consultancy services as well as other services. The purchaser of a turnkey system will need to be assured that it exactly fits his requirements, as technically individual computing needs vary greatly.

Software houses

These businesses rent or sell to firms needing them programs for routine procedures, such as credit control, or special ones, such as a sophisticated analysis of investment programs. Software facilities are sometimes available from bureaux offering general services.

Time sharing

A factor that has encouraged the growth of supporting services in business computing has been the increase in numbers of main-frame computers. Rarely will a main-frame computer be used to its full potential from the moment of installation, and often the user's demand will never reach the maximum capacity. As computers are expensive to purchase, install, run and maintain, the owners will have a strong incentive to sell spare time. The growth of data transmission facilities has increased this incentive. A whole branch of the service industry, known as *time-brokers*, now specialise in this work, although some bureaux undertake it with their other functions.

Location and use of hardware

In some arrangements, the bureau will provide the computer on the user's premises, as well as the software and staff; alternatively the user will provide these. Another arrangement is for the client to provide the software and his staff to use it on the bureau's premises. A common arrangement is for the client to have his own terminals which are served by the bureau's computer on a time-sharing basis. Individual jobs can be done, or large numbers of similar operations can be performed, by *remote batch processing*.

Other bureau services

Some bureaux prepare documents for processing. In early days, this meant card-punching or tape-recording. Either the bureau or the client would pick up the work and return it. Today, some bureaux will transform documents into MICR form (see p. 59) and process them. When printed sheets roll off a computer, they often need to be 'bursted' (separated from one another), the edges need to be trimmed off, and the separated sheets need to be 'collated', i.e. put into proper order, and bound into miniature book form. Some bureaux offer these services. Some bureaux will provide training courses for users' staff. Computer appreciation courses will prepare people who will be affected by the coming of a new system, e.g. management, accountants, store-keepers and clerks. Other courses may train staff in technical work, such as operating computers or applying them to business situations.

Obtaining a computer

A firm requiring a computer may purchase it outright if it has adequate capital resources. More probably, it will use the services of a bank or other financial institution. Outright purchase will have the advantage of incurring just one major item of expenditure. Unaided purchase is likely, in the long run, to be the cheapest method of acquisition. Purchase through a bank-loan will be more expensive because of interest charges. Purchase will leave the user free to use, and if need be to extend, the computer. It can of course sell the computer at any time, and purchase a new one. A relevant but not completely predictable factor is the rate of obsolescence. This will determine the trade-in price of an old computer, and under some conditions the owners could be at a disadvantage when compared with users who were not owners. This problem will not affect users who rent their computers. Renting, however, is more expensive and the machine never becomes the user's property. If the user's business runs into financial difficulty, the computer may be repossessed and the situation becomes very much worse.

Leasing requires contracting to take a computer over a longer period than renting, and to that extent the arrangement is less flexible than renting. On the other hand, the charges are likely to be less than with renting. When the lease runs out, renewal may be at a lower rate. In some arrangements, in renegotiating a lease for a new computer allowance may be made for the value of the old computer. Whereas some renting agreements require extra payment to be made for use of the new computer beyond a set time, leasing agreements carry no restrictions.

The use of computer bureaux

The services of computer bureaux offer various advantages to firms which have their own computer systems. Some computer users find that their systems can cope with the normal flow of work, yet equipment and staff are periodically overloaded, e.g. at annual stocktaking, or a quarterly analysis of sales. This extra work can most economically be put out to a bureau. Bureau services can also be useful in particular one-off situations, e.g. where a social services organisation decides to computerise thousands of client records, setting up computer files to replace a manual system. Another kind of arrangement is for a bureau to provide stand-by services where the client uses facilities in the event of an emergency, such as would occur if their computer broke down or some records were destroyed by fire.

Where a bureau offers the use of its computer to clients, the service may be very valuable if a firm is going over to a computer system and needs the opportunity for its staff to gain experience in using a computer and software.

Use of a bureau obviously increases a computer user's costs. Another disadvantage is that documents sent to a bureau will be unavailable for the time being to the firm. Security will be less, and strict privacy cannot be maintained. The client will have less control over the accuracy and standard of presentation of output. A strict contract could ensure that work was returned to time, and delay attracted penalties, but in general, a client might well find that at times the standard of punctuality was lower when the work was out than when it was done on the premises.

Arrangements between bureau and client

Work undertaken by the bureau should be subject to a clear, detailed, written agreement. The cost should be stated. This can be at a fixed price for a particular job. Another basis is the volume of work to be done. Some bureaux charge according to the time it takes to link up and disconnect, because with a main-frame computer processing time may be an insignificant fraction of the whole. In some operations, transmission charges will be added. As with electricity supply, computer time in off-peak periods may be cheaper. Where a user may wish to avoid running up too great a bill, he may agree to an arrangement where the service is cut off when cost reaches a predetermined level. Economy can be secured if two or more users form a consortium to negotiate with a bureau, although the individual may lose some independence.

Principles of costings

A distinction must be made between *effectiveness* and *efficiency*. Two processing systems may be equally effective, i.e. they may both process a batch of documents equally well. But efficiency relates performance to cost, so that if the first costs £0.85 per invoice, and the second £0.67, then the latter is the more efficient.

Firms will often have to decide whether to put work out or whether to do it themselves on their own premises, and in this case, which of alternative systems to use. A sound decision will weigh carefully the balance between the costs incurred and the benefits obtained.

Tangible costs will include the cost of outright purchase of a computer and peripherals, or obtaining their services in another way. It will be necessary to engage new specialised staff and to retrain some existing staff. Software will need to be bought in, hired or written by the firm's own programmers. Installing a main-frame computer will mean preparing the site, providing air-conditioning, and with most systems, laying transmission lines. Costs less easy to calculate will be the management time devoted to running the new system.

Most computer systems are introduced in the hope of bringing obvious benefits such as reduction in work-force and the speeding up of systems. Other benefits which may come, but are more difficult to assess, are better decision-making through better management information, more enlightened forecasting and budgeting, and the exercise of greater control over the whole operation of the business.

Short questions

1 A road haulage firm which processes its data on manual systems has enquired about conversion to a computerised system, and has been offered a turnkey system. Explain what this would mean in relationship to this business, and give two arguments against accepting this method of meeting its needs.

2 Outline the ways in which computer bureaux can help a firm, distinguishing between services provided on the bureau's own premises and those provided elsewhere.

3 A local authority has an old small computer, which already carries its maximum load. It needs to extend the scope of its computerisation, and is considering acquiring a larger, more up-to-date, main-frame computer, either by outright purchase or renting or leasing. What information should it take into account before reaching a decision between these alternatives?

4 A firm wishes to have its pay-roll work undertaken by a computer bureau, and asks for tenders from several bureaux. Discuss whether it should necessarily accept the lowest tender for the work.

5 Explain the difference between the terms 'effective' and 'efficient' when applied to computing. Explain why the possibility of indirect benefits and indirect costs complicates the measurement of efficiency.

Practical work

1 (a) From your local *Yellow Pages*, list all the headings printed in red with

'Computer(s)';
'Data';
'Information'.

(b) Taking into account line entries and larger advertisements, and by making personal enquiries if need be, describe briefly the kind of work undertaken by the organisations grouped in the separate headings.

(c) Give examples of firms covered by your survey: (i) which are computer bureaux; (ii) which are not computer bureaux.

2 Using *Yellow Pages*, other directories if need be and your own local knowledge, give the names and addresses of firms which could meet the following needs:

(a) Provide stationery for a main-frame computer which was running short.

(b) Provide the services for three months of a computer programmer needed to transfer large quantities of information held under a manual system or to computer files.

(c) Give preliminary information about installing a minicomputer.

(d) Give a quotation for a bulk order of floppy disks for use in a new microcomputer system.

(e) Give professional advice to a large charitable organisation on whether to computerise its records, and if so how to go about it.

(f) Provide a remote-entry batch-processing system for a business which sends out large numbers of invoices each quarter.

(g) Perform urgent minor repairs to two VDUs which have broken down.

If possible, try to discover whether the services can be obtained at the address given or whether the organisation has to communicate with someone else.

Questions relevant to BTEC written examinations

1 Describe *four* different services which a computer bureau can provide for a business. State in each case the extent to which the staff of the business will be involved.

2 (a) Describe important points to be settled by a firm or organisation if it is to use the services of a computer bureau.

(b) A firm wishes to obtain the services of a main-frame computer. Explain the alternatives to direct purchase.

Other examination questions

1 (A) Describe the services commonly provided by computer bureaux.

(B) Discuss the factors to be considered when deciding whether to use a bureau rather than in-house facilities. (IMS – Information Systems I, June 1985)

2 Discuss the usefulness of a computer bureau in overcoming some of the problems of systems conversion. (IMS – Computer Project Planning and Control, June 1984)

10 SOFTWARE

> This chapter
>
> - describes software;
> - explains levels in computer language;
> - describes the purposes of compilers, assemblers and interpreters;
> - explains the structure of programs;
> - distinguishes between operating and utility software;
> - describes and illustrates packages and criteria for judging them.

Languages and levels

Chapter 1 described the start of a data and information processing operation. Both the steps to be taken and the data to be used were stated in English and readily understandable by management and employees concerned with the matter. By the time the messages reached the computer, they would be expressed as a large number of binary digits and it would need an expert to read them with the same accuracy and fluency that a person of normal literacy could read their originals. What the computer receives are instructions needed to carry out the intentions of its masters. The collective name given to these organised sets of commands is *software*, and it mainly consists of programs written from outside the system; but it also includes instructions which are implanted in various pieces of hardware at the time of manufacture.

The gentlest method of transferring business and similar expressions to a computer is to express them in a language which is closely linked to English; the most popular is undoubtedly BASIC, in one of its several forms. Working examples will appear later in Chapter 15, but mention of some of the words used in this language, such as PRINT, READ and GOTO, which approximate closely to human imperatives, show the ease of transition at this stage. This and other languages with strong relationships to written English are called *high-level*. The final instructions which work the computer are in *machine language*, and such languages are said to be *low-level*.

When human beings converse with one another the language is common, so that instructions like 'start the car' or 'lay the table for dinner' are easily understood, since the receiver is likely to be aware of the compendious nature of the direction. Starting the car will be naturally assumed to include checking that the gear is in neutral, turning the ignition key, using the choke if necessary, releasing the brake and engaging the gear, and depressing the throttle. Unfortunately, before a computer will respond properly to a human direction, it needs to be given the minutest detail. Several standard methods may be used to bridge this communication gap.

Compilers, assemblers and interpreters

When a manufacturer supplies a computer, he may well supply a *compiler*, a program which bridges this gap by translating the original program (known as the *source program*), e.g. instructions in BASIC, into the required program in machine language known as the *object program*. By *compiling*, the term used to describe this process, a complete new program has been produced, which can be kept stored on the computer or run on to a portable store, so that it can be used again for the particular process in question, e.g. setting departmental budget targets. Besides translating from the high-level language, a compiler will detect errors in programs and reveal them in print. A compiler is complicated and expensive, for it must cope with the large number of different processes which a high-level language can initiate; an added difficulty may be the variety of forms in which the high-level language, such as BASIC, has developed, given that a particular language may be improved in the light of experience and modified to accommodate developments in hardware. A main-frame computer will be at its most useful when through compilation it can receive input in a variety of languages, so that compilation may involve a large amount of software.

An alternative is to write the program in *assembly language*, at a level between high and low but near machine language. This is easier to understand and write than machine code, as code forms are used, e.g. LDX means 'load', i.e. put into a register. An *assembler* then conveys the assembly-language instructions to the computer as the compiler does with a high-level language program. The object program thus created can be recorded and stored for re-use.

Another way of using high-level language is to use a special program called an *interpreter*. This is fed into the computer, followed by the source program. Each original instruction is translated and straight away executed by the computer. The method is slower than the others, and no object program is created for storage and future use. A balancing advantage is that little computer storage space is required, so that interpeters are increasingly used for microcomputers.

Program construction

Some computer programs contain just a few instructions, are quite short and can be represented by a single short straight line. A program to add two quantities together and to print-out or store the total would be an example. Very much more is likely to be needed in the computerisation of a business system. The invoicing of a transaction has implications for ledger accounts, for the sale department, for stock systems and possibly for representatives paid on commission. If an overall program is used, a large number of instructions will be needed, and they will form not one short straight line, but an intricate pattern of branches and loops, each connected at least once with a long line. More than one programmer may contribute, each writing a group of related instructions which, with a few alterations, could operate independently as a program. Such groups are *modules* and the program construction is *modular*. Supposing further information were needed in future from the invoices, e.g. relating to sizes of orders or seasonal trends, other modules could be added.

In data and information processing certain calculations are likely to be used very often, as part of larger processes. A firm selling a number of commodities may wish to calculate the average rate of turnover for each, i.e.

$$\frac{\text{Cost of sales}}{\frac{1}{2}(\text{Opening stock} + \text{Closing stock})}$$

This could be done for each commodity by introducing a *sub-routine* into the program. The main program could be concerned with overall sales analysis, according to territory, commodity, profitability,· etc. At a suitable point in the program, a loop would be introduced which would calculate for each commodity the rate of turnover, and store it pending the final print-out, after which the program would end or continue with the remaining processes. For example, it could print out products in order of profitability.

Operational software

Computers used in information processing are usually part of a system ranging from the simplest, which merely connects the computer to a printer or VDU, to the most complex, where a number of computers and peripherals form a network stretching hundreds of miles. *Operational software* is needed to control the working of computer systems, large and small, and a number of different programs will be needed, each with a specialised function.

Essential movements for multiprogramming, described in Chapter 7, are an important function of operational software. Another function is allocation of priority where a computer has two or more input links. Operational software is needed to co-ordinate the working of a computer's main store with its backing store. When undertaking a particular job, software will be needed to make the most efficient use of the resources of the system.

Although computer systems enjoy a high degree of automation, for that is their essential nature, they must allow for some human control through the console of the main-frame or the keyboard of the VDU terminal. These arrangements are made through operational software. The activities of a main-frame computer need to be carefully logged by the computer itself, in addition to manual records of its use which user's staff may keep as routine. One reason is to ensure efficient running, but equally important is the need to guard against deliberate misuse, breach of security and violation of privacy. Again, special software provides this service.

Programs for all these purposes are often written in a special language.

Utility software

Some relatively simple routines are required in the working of most computer systems: data is transferred from magnetic disks or tapes to files, and back again; files need to be sorted or their contents copied; tapes need to be labelled; and data has, from time to time, to be cleared from storage. Procedures are comparatively simple, and the program for carrying them out is called *utility software*.

Packages

Programs so far described in this chapter have been general ones, in that they are used in nearly all computer systems, and do not relate to the kind of business being undertaken. Most computer users, however, will need in addition computer programs for specialised work relating to the business. An examining board may computerise the system for entering candidates, sending lists to examiners and recording marks. A factory may use a computer to improve the security of its stock system, speed up stock-handling, rationalise stock-taking and apply operational research methods to its stock-holding policy. An authority owning a large number of council houses may use a computer system for recording rents and processing repair work. These are just a few examples of computer users whose software needs can be met by purchasing or hiring *packages*. These are sets of computer programs drawn up by experts outside the organisation concerned, to meet particular needs. The packages, which are sometimes called *application packages*, consist of a suite of programs in the form of disks, cards or written statements, together with documentation. This consists of supporting charts, instructions for use and information about the suitability of the programs in various situations. Where packages are obtained free from the computer manufacturer, they are called *bundled*. Packages which have to be paid for, e.g. when obtained through a software house, are called *unbundled*. The package market, in broad terms, covers particular types of package, e.g. for pay-roll or ledger accounting, or particular kinds of client, e.g. stockbrokers or building societies.

Packages offer to users various advantages. They are likely to embody a great deal more practical experience than is available to an individual user. Chapter 15 will demonstrate why the production of a good program may be a long and complicated process. The user of a package can use it straight away, with all the documentation needed. Where a standard package is widely used, costs will have the advantage of large-scale production; furthermore, in common applications such as pay-roll or invoicing, competition between producers may be keen. However, packaging has disadvantages. Businesses and organisations vary greatly in the details of their procedures and the machines and equipment used, even when general terms such as 'billing' or 'ledger accounting' or 'listing' describe them. A package may need individual alteration to run successfully in a particular system, so that cost will increase. Some manufacturers and software houses will write packages completely to a single customer's requirements, but this is even more expensive. To be effective, a package must foresee all the idiosyncracies of a particular system, and it is sometimes better to engage full-time or temporary professional staff, rather than acquire a package from outside.

A user considering a package will need to take into account a number of points. Business systems are apt to change from time to time, to improve efficiency or to adjust to environmental changes. The user will need to know how the application of the package will be affected, and if changes are needed, who will be responsible. Other factors are the demand for main and backing store under various input loads, and the varying times the package will take to run.

Short questions

1 Explain:
   (a) the term 'level' applied to computer languages;
   (b) why one computer system may use more than one level of languages.

2 Explain the difference between the terms compiler, assembler, and interpreter by drawing simple sketches and writing brief notes.

3 A firm which manufactures and sells goods uses a package to produce invoices which are sent to customers, to provide routine data for various departments and to produce management reports. Most of the object uses of the package are achieved in a long, complicated program.
   (a) State the main modules you would expect to find in the program, giving a summary of what each module does.
   (b) Select one of these modules and use it to illustrate the terms:
      (i) input data;
      (ii) output data;
      (iii) document (other than invoice).

4 The following are the names of sub-routines used in various computer programs:
   (i) currency conversion;
   (ii) overtime payment calculations;
   (iii) postage for first- and second-class mail.
   (a) Describe for each sub-routine operations you would expect it to carry out.
   (b) Give one example for each sub-routine of a program in which it could be usefully included.

5 (a) Explain to an office worker who has only a general idea of the meaning of software the difference between operation and utility software.
   (b) Apply your classification with reasons to each of the following:
   (i) a program which connected one of three microcomputers at any given time to a single main-frame computer with which they formed a complete system;
   (ii) a program which produced pass-list data from thousands of computerised examination results.

6 A software firm sells packages to house and estate agents for use in their daily work. Each contains several programs.
   (a) Suggest in general terms what each program might do.
   (b) Give examples of items of data which an agent would put into a microcomputer when using one of the programs.
   (c) One or more of the programs in the package could provide management information. Give two different examples of such information which would help the agent.
   (d) Explain briefly why the package would be likely to contain more than these programs.

Practical work

1 Study a club, business or other organisation which you know personally, but which does not use a computer. Assume that it went over to computer, had provided the hardware, and wished to provide programs from outside. Obtain information about appropriate packages to be used in a new system, such as what they would do, how they would be used, how the old system would be changed, etc.

2 From local computer users, obtain examples of:
   (a) packages in use;
   (b) programs produced by users and not bought or hired;
   (c) sub-routines in use in (a) or (b).
   Note any difference between the experiences of users who use packages and those who do not.

Questions relevant to BTEC written examinations

1 (a) What is a computer language?

(b) Why are so many different languages available in computing today?

(c) Give examples of languages often used in business processing, and explain why in one piece of processing languages of different level may be used.

2 (a) Give examples of two different packages designed for business, and explain what each does.

(b) What will a user take into account in choosing between two packages from different suppliers, but both claiming in a general way to undertake the same kind of work?

(c) What is the alternative for a computer user who wishes to program his computer without acquiring a package, and what advantages could this arrangement bring?

Other examination questions

1 Explain what is meant by:
   (i) utility software;
   (ii) application package.
What are the main advantages to be gained by the users from the adoption of application packages? (AAT – Data Processing, June 1983)

2 The availability and reducing real costs of microcomputers mean that more and more organisations are purchasing these machines. Many of these organisations, particularly the smaller ones, lack the expertise to write their own programs, and rely on being able to buy suitable software packages from software houses or the manufacturers.

You are required to list and briefly explain:

(a) the type of information you should have available *before* approaching the software suppliers; and

(b) the factors involved in deciding whether or not to select a particular package.
(ICMA – Management Information Systems and Data Processing II, May 1984)

11 STAFF AND DEPARTMENTS

> This chapter
> - describes the work of specialised staff responsible for data preparation, computer operation, systems analysis and programming;
> - describes entry standards, personal qualities and career prospects for such staff;
> - describes the organisation of staff into departments.

Processing departments

In the simplest applications of computers to businesses and organisations one person only, often the owner, will perform all the operations needed in using the computer and peripherals for processing, and may even write simple programs in a high-level language to extend the scope of the system beyond the limits of software provided by the manufacturer or obtained from a software house. For more extensive processing demands, more than one specialist is likely to be employed, labour will be divided, and two or more sections of the kind described below will form a distinguishable department called the computer department, the data-processing department or the information-processing department, to give the usual titles. Sometimes, the historical birthplace of the computing function is still used, so that an accounting department or administration department will include what is virtually an autonomous processing department. In the largest processing units a diversity of professional and technical skills will be found, and a carefully planned organisational structural and smooth running lines of communication will be needed if the parent body is to be best served by the new technology. The divisions of activities and personnel described in this chapter are intended to give a broad survey, with a more detailed analysis of procedures and problems to follow in Chapter 12.

Data preparation

In early days, data was usually input to computer systems as punched cards or paper tape, from source documents, and verification procedures were necessary to ensure that coded input was correct. The specialised work and the heavy equipment needed soon justified the creation of a separate *data-preparation department*. The demand for punching processes is rapidly declining, but preparation in new ways is still needed, as a great volume of input is from source documents which need some intermediate process before their data can enter the computer. Punching machinery is therefore giving way to key-to-disk and key-to-magnetic tape stations. Visual and other means of validation are a stage in data preparation, and wrong documents or inadequately completed ones must be prevented from entering the system. Preparation may include transforming data which is electronically unreadable into a form which is. The code on a cheque will readily identify the originating bank, branch and account number, but under present arrangements the amount which the customer writes down must be coded in some way if the system is to debit his account and credit the payee's. Efficient batch processing, already described in Chapter 7, will need careful checking and organisation, and the data-preparation department will see to this. Input is likely to come from computer files as well as from documents and, where a number of files are in use, care of them and updating will require the departmental staff to include a *file librarian*.

Staff in the department will usually be at the levels of clerk, controller or supervisor. The basic work of preparing data calls for ability to work on repetitive processes with speed and accuracy, and a good operator will be able to adapt quickly to new machinery and situations. Qualities required are those of a good typist. Recruitment is often at modest GCSE standard, including English. Training is usually given, with prospects for promotion within the department and possibly in the computer operating and programming departments later.

Computer operating department

The centre of any sizeable computing system is likely to be a main-frame computer operated from a console by a trained operator. He will control in a general way through his keyboard the input, processing and output of data, although the detailed activities will be determined by the operating system and application software. He will need to know how to start up the computer, and will keep a careful record of the progress of each job through the computer, tracking down errors. He will be concerned with routine maintenance, cleaning and securing a dust and damp-free atmosphere through the proper working of the air-conditioner. For serious breakdowns, the manufacturer's experts must be speedily brought in. The department will probably be responsible for all hardware, such as key stations and microcomputers linked to the system. In small departments, the operator may combine his main duties with some programming or other functions. In a large and busy department, he may be helped by junior operators who perform ancillary tasks such as loading tapes on to drives or bursting and decollating stationery at output. Large departments will be needed where more than one main-frame is in use. Where the computer is in continuous use, the work will be organised into shifts. A common arrangement is to have three eight-hour shifts, with staff times overlapping to allow the old shift to hand over to the new. To run larger systems, a hierarchy of operations will develop, with shift leader and service operator being common appointments.

```
                    JOB DESCRIPTION

Title:    Computer Operator

Responsibilities:   the operator is required to supervise the running of
                    the computer installation and to operate, where
                    necessary, the individual pieces of equipment.

                    Specific tasks include:

                    - powering up the equipment
                    - loading the system
                    - loading, replenishing and unloading peripherals as
                      necessary
                    - observing and acting upon messages received from
                      the computer's operating system via the operator's
                      own console display screen
                    - monitoring and logging the performance of the
                      computer
                    - monitoring quality of printed results by observation
                    - cleaning on a regular basis equipment sensitive
                      to dust
                    - checking the performance of airconditioning units
                      required to control the working environment and
                      any other tasks which may arise within the main
                      objectives.
```

Fig. 11.1 Job description of a computer operator

Computer operators are often recruited at GCSE standard, but usually at higher levels than for the data preparation department. English and mathematics are desirable subjects and new entrants often have GCE 'A'-level passes. Manufacturers sometimes offer training courses and operators from time to time need updating on changing hardware and software techniques. In temperament, they need to be capable of working under pressure and of reacting quickly and effectively to the periodical crises which beset most computer systems.

Experience in computer operating is often a first step in a career as a computer programmer.

Systems analysis department

The brief accounts of data preparation and computer operating just given have, of course, assumed that a computer system has been installed and is working satisfactorily. Transforming a manual business system to this stage is likely to involve a great amount of highly technical work; Chapter 14 describes in some detail the stages of a typical computer installation. The systems analyst occupies a key position in bringing the new system into being. First, an objective investigation into the old system must be made, followed by an analysis of the organisation and activities. This will take in procedures, personnel and documents. Next a computer-based system will be designed, which will include a description of the hardware to be obtained, the software to go with it, and the inevitable changes in numbers and status of staff and their work. The final stage will be implementing the new scheme, which means planning a smooth efficient transition from the old system to the new. Systems analysts will be concerned with all four stages.

In a small organisation, a single analyst may do everything required, but where there is work for more than one, a degree of division of labour and some specialisation may occur, with investigation and analysis occupying one analyst and team, and design and implementation another. Once a computer system is established, systems analysts are still likely to be needed: existing systems will need to be adjusted to changing conditions, and new applications of computing sought. Again, division of labour and specialisation tend to develop. In large undertakings, systems analysts usually work in teams, and a vertical organisation structure grows with senior supervisory analysts and junior trainee ones.

A good analyst will have a wide knowledge. He must understand how businesses and organisations run, and be an expert on documents and paperwork generally. As he will be recommending the purchase and use of hardware and software, he must be well acquainted with its acquisition and installation. It will be unusual for a systems analyst to be employed without at least one programmer being employed as well; but the analyst must know at least the rudiments of programming if communication is to be good. In investigating a system, he will need some skill in interviewing techniques.

Systems analysis requires special personal characteristics. The analyst may need to throw initial light on the work of people who may be made redundant, or given lower status when the scheme is set up; he must therefore be tactful, shrewd and persistent. His work will bring him into touch with other professionals, both in computing and other fields, such as management and accounting. The emergence of a sound new system may depend largely on his ability to communicate clearly and simply, and on his persuasiveness. As his title suggests, analytical ability of a high order is needed.

With such demanding personal requirements, entrants to the systems analysis branch of the profession are often graduates, or holders of business diplomas or foundation qualifications in computing. A minimum standard of GCE 'A'-level is desirable, with mathematics a useful subject. Career prospects are good within the larger systems analysis departments, and experience within is sometimes a helpful step to more senior and general appointments outside.

Programming department

When the systems analyst's work has ended, the programmer's begins. The analyst will have specified clearly in English statements what data is to be put into the computer, what is to be done with it inside, and how it is to be output. If the task is simple and limited, one program will suffice; otherwise, the equivalent of two or more programs will be needed. An alternative is to make the program modular, dividing the work between two or more programmers. Application programs, i.e. those carrying out office or similar procedures, will be written in a high-level language, while operating programs, which control the working of the system, are likely to be in low-level language. The programmer will, of course, test-run the program and correct mistakes. He will prepare documentation for users. Besides writing new programs, in a large organisation a programmer may be working on maintenance, which includes improving programs and modifying them to meet changes in the business systems which they serve.

Good programming is the work of an analytical and logical mind, and employers look for a GCE 'A'-level standard of education and often take on graduates. GCSE (or students with 'O'-level) standards in English and mathematics are desirable. A programmer can expect to be working in several computer languages, and most employers offer training courses. In the simplest situation one person may be responsible for both systems analysis and programming. On the other hand, work may be so extensive that programmers are arranged in project teams, offering a career structure of entry at junior or trainee programmer through senior programmer to project leader and ultimately to chief programmer. Some programmers move from programming to systems analysis, for which their first skills are a good foundation.

A good programmer should be able to work as a team member with colleagues in his own department and with those, such as systems analysts, outside. However, sociability is less important than with system analysts. Writing programs and associated software demands great mental concentration which is best achieved when the programmer works in isolation.

Short questions

1   A businessman uses a microcomputer with a VDU, printer and disk-drive to help him run his business. He uses these devices single-handed. Draw up two wide columns. In the left-hand one state the activities occurring in the main departments mentioned in this chapter, in the right-hand column whether the businessman performs the activity, and if so how he does it.

Staff and departments **117**

2   A firm of publishers has a large data preparation department. Give an example of each of the following which you could expect to find in the department:
   (a) an electronic device, stating its purpose;
   (b) a routine being carried out by one of the staff;
   (c) a document, stating why it was in the department.

3   A computer operator works a main-frame computer at the head office of a multiple-shop firm with branches throughout the UK.
   (a) Give an example of one piece of routine work he would carry out.
   (b) Give an example of an emergency that could occur in the system, and how he might cope with it.

4   A computer department operates in shifts, the team for a new shift overlapping for a short time the old shift. What would you expect to happen at the overlap?

5   Why, in your view, is a pass in GCSE English important, and a pass in mathematics desirable for entrants to the computing profession?

6   (a) State the four main headings used to describe a systems analyst's work.
   (b) State for each the kind of people with whom he could be expected to work.

7   (a) After revising earlier work on systems, explain what is meant by 'systems' in 'systems analyst'.
   (b) Does an analyst undertake any important work other than analysis?

8   Explain why some people make better systems analysts than programmers, while others make better programmers than analysts.

9   (a) List the main tasks likely to be performed in a programming department.
   (b) State which you think would be the most difficult, giving reasons for your choice.

10   A friend who has not yet started a career has basic qualifications which would enable him to enter any branch of the computing profession, but is uncertain which to choose. Write brief headed notes to help him decide.

Practical work

1   Study advertisements for vacancies in computing work displayed in newspapers, magazines, employment agencies, etc. Summarise the vacancies on a broadsheet under these, and if need be, other headings:
   Name of post;
   Name of employer;
   Employer's business;
   Salary;
   Working conditions;
   Prospects;
   Entry requirements.

Try to cover as many of the posts mentioned in the chapter as possible.

What points of interest are revealed by your broad survey? (*Note:* Given sufficient local resources, the field of study could be sub-divided, and the project could be done by a team of students.)

2   Some public examinations cover mainly subjects in computing, some include computing and selected subjects. Obtain information about the computing content of both types of examination. You are advised that syllabuses under the following headings are relevant:

  Computing;
  Computer studies;
  Data processing;
  Information processing;
  Systems analysis;
  Computer science;

and you may find others.

Remember to include local institutions of further education.

Show how success in particular examinations would relate to careers in different branches of computing.

Questions relevant to BTEC written examination

1   Describe the work of the data preparation department of a large firm mentioning the different forms of input to the department, the machinery and other devices used, and contacts with other computing staff outside the department.

2   (*a*) Describe the work of a large systems analysis department, giving examples of group and individual responsibilities within the department.

(*b*) Explain why good relationships between this department and the programming department are essential for the efficiency of information processing.

Other examination questions

1   (*a*) What are the human aspects of the systems analyst's job and why are they important?

(*b*) How are they taken into account in analysing and designing a computer-based information system? (IDPM – Systems Analysis and Design 1, Dec. 1985)

2   Discuss the relationships within a data processing organisation between

  data preparation
  operating
  programming
  systems analysis.

(IMS – Information Systems 1, Nov. 1984)

3 (a) List *four* of the duties of a computer operator in a large computer installation.

(b) In a small computer installation the computer operators frequently operate ancillary machinery to handle output from the printer. Name *two* such machines and describe their purpose.

(c) In large Data Processing Departments some staff may be organised into project teams. Name *two* types of personnel that may be found in a project team and state *one* advantage of such teams when compared with the traditional staff structure.
(RSA – June 1985)

12 THE ELECTRONIC OFFICE AND ITS SETTING

> This chapter
> - describes the coming of the electronic office;
> - explains how the following devices and systems are being used in business and organisations today: word processors, telex, facsimile transmission, electronic post and mail, electronic funds transfer, information recording and retrieval, teletype, videotex, teletext, viewdata, electronic conferencing and calendars.

The office and electronics

Earlier chapters in this book have described the benefits brought by the introduction of computerised methods to the running of businesses and other organisations: manpower has been reduced, routines have been accelerated and the quality of output has been improved; and often new information has been produced to help management in decision making. Evident though these benefits have been, new problems are arising which will only be solved when electronic applications are carried much further. The main needs now are to make the handling of data as speedy as its processing, to reduce physically the growing volume of paper which has to be transmitted and ultimately stored and to improve the methods by which data travels inside the office and between offices and the world outside. The changes which are occurring are seen, not only in computers and their peripherals, but in the coming of an almost unending series of new devices and procedures. Some are, by definition, computers of a specialised kind, but some are not. The whole trend is towards the establishment of the *electronic office*. This is not a fixed concept, but an ideal in which the work which used to be done by clerks with some help from mechanised and electrical devices is taken over by computers and other electronic devices, with human involvement at a minimum. With these changes came developments in internal and external communications carrying messages in digital, written, spoken and graphic form. The role of the state and the recently privatised sector in these forms of transmission are outlined in Chapter 13.

Word processors

An important stage in the change has taken the commonest piece of office machinery, the typewriter, from the original manual model, entirely reliant upon manpower (or womanpower) through the less taxing electrical typewriter to the *word processor*, a typewriter with new electronic facilities.

On a manual model the standard of output depends upon the skill with which the typist performs a number of separate operations: paper and carbon must be correctly fed and centred into the machine, margins set and observed, paragraphs indented, individual lines typed to the correct length, with words sub-divided correctly. Keys must be tapped evenly at the correct pressure, and spaces, hyphens, punctuation marks and underscoring must be correctly inserted. The whole lay-out, including any tabulation, must be pleasing to the eye. Where photographs, diagrams and similar material are to be inserted in the text, the space must be planned. Words must be spelt according to the dictionary. Errors must be detected as soon as possible and corrected as unobtrusively as possible.

Word processors vary in their complexity and facilities. The simplest will bring electronic aid to the operator in several of the routine tasks just described; some word processors are capable of all of them, and when connected to specialised systems, individually or linked to other word processors, they are capable of rather more. Before one or more word processors are installed to replace conventional typewriters, a careful study is needed as, like computers, their cost-effectiveness depends upon carrying an adequate workload and working with other devices in a purpose-designed system.

In the commonest type of word processor, information will be typed on a keyboard with a light touch, will appear on visual display and will be stored in a digital form on a floppy disk. Printing need not occur until the operator is satisfied with the appearance of the information, and this can be judged from display. Errors can be corrected by inserting omitted material or deleting erroneous material and replacing it with the correct information. The extent of the amendment can be a single letter or figure or whole lines and passages.

Study of business letters and other documents prepared on typewriters will often reveal commonly used phrases, such as 'We regret that we are unable to offer you the appointment for which you applied' or 'Car allowance will be at 22p per mile for the first 300 miles, and 18p per mile thereafter'. Some word processors hold stock phrases on store so that they can be included in a piece of work at the touch of a single key. Another facility enables a prepared piece of work, which suits a particular situation to be reworded, *mutatis mutandi*, to meet another, e.g. a statement about conditions of employment may refer to 'senior staff' being allowed 'four weeks' paid holiday a year and earning a salary of '£8,000 per year', with some of the quoted phrases occurring more than once in the document. A copy of the

Fig. 12.1 Word processor (*by courtesy of Vickers Furniture*)

document may be adjusted to describe the conditions for junior staff by searching automatically for the occurrence of a term in column 1 and replacing it by the term in column 2.

Column 1	*Column 2*
senior staff	junior staff
four weeks	two weeks
£8,000 per year	£5,000 per year

Most word processors are capable of formatting, i.e. arranging the work in the style required, in the way that a good typist would on a manual machine. Formatting often includes *justification*, i.e. adjusting the spacing of letters and words to equalise line lengths so that the margins appear straight, as in a printed book. Some processors can store thousands of correctly spelt words, check each word keyed in, and draw attention to any discrepancies. Documents in information processing often need to show graphs, charts and diagrams. An advanced word processor may have the facility to prepare graphic work and insert it at the correct point as the text is prepared, or prepare and insert it later. The principle is digital conversion. For simple items such as bar-charts, the software is fairly simple, but for a detailed graphic image it is complicated, and reproduction on this principle is necessarily restricted.

The main facilities of word processors are given above. But there are others, and a specialised book would be needed to give a comprehensive and detailed account of the full range.

Powerful as a word processor standing alone may be, it becomes even more powerful when working in circuit with other word processors or electronic devices. A *communicating word processor* is designed to work in such situations. Where the whole system lies within one organisation, such as a factory with offices and warehouses on the same site, connection is by a local *network*. Word processors may also use outside networks, described in Chapter 13.

Two or more processors may share the same printer, which may be more powerful than that provided with an individual model. The extra facilities which distinguish a word processor from an ordinary typewriter are owed to computer power. A *shared-logic* system links word processors to a computer giving facilities which it would be uneconomical to provide on an individual basis.

Normally, a typist will prepare correspondence and other text from written drafts, from live dictation or by listening to a dictaphone. Usually, the dictator is in an office, as is the typist. A modern system enables the businessman to dictate a message, which is conveyed by phone to a tape in the typist's home or office. The document can be prepared by the typist, and transmitted in digital form back to the originator for checking or on to a third location for action.

The general advantages which a word processor offers over a typewriter is the ease with which corrections can be made, and copies run off, and the improvement in quality in the finished work because the operator can see how the text will appear before committing it to paper.

Telex

The term comes from the contraction of the words 'teleprinter' and 'exchange'. A teleprinter is a typewriter designed so that the output can be conveyed to another teleprinter through a telephone transmission, or other line. The message to be sent out is typed, travels along the line and is typed out at the other end. At the transmitting end of the line is a *modem* which modulates the typewriter output into impulses suitable for transmission. A second modem at the receiving end of the line demodulates the impulses so that the message is typed out on the receiver's typewriter. Before computing was used for the processing of information, national and international systems were well developed, serving both business and military purposes. Typical uses would be by a manufacturer in Birmingham despatching a written description of the numbers and types of products held in stock available to meet an order from a London agent, or a shipping agent in

Fig. 12.2 Telex machine (*by courtesy of British Telecom*)

Liverpool advising a Marseilles merchant of a consignment of goods due to arrive next day. The system served the purpose of a telephone link, with the advantage of input and output being in writing.

Much information is still conveyed by the telex system, but with much greater efficiency than in earlier days. The underlying communication network has been greatly extended. The first telex machines were noisy and slow in action, input and output were tedious and transmission techniques, by today's standards, were cumbersome. Working speeds have been very much increased, and whereas specialised training used to be needed by operators, on some modern machines a high degree of automation occurs and a trained typist can soon master a teleprinter. In earlier systems, along any given line, a message could only travel in one direction at one time. Today, simultaneous transmission and reception are possible, because large quantities of data can be stored before transmission or afterwards. This means that a message can be received by an unattended teleprinter, or left on store and despatched when a line is clear or when low off-peak charges apply. Some teleprinters have convenient immobilising devices to guard against unauthorised use. Press-button calling devices make for speed and simplicity in use. The general movement towards integrating electronic office devices is seen in teleprinters which can be linked with typewriters, word processors and desk-top computers. A modern teleprinter is still not a computer in the strict sense, but it can now be controlled by a microcomputer in a way which enhances its usefulness and benefits the system of which it is part.

Facsimile transmission

In business today a document, plan or diagram may be needed so urgently that normal mail transmission is too slow. A firm's lawyer in West Germany may require sight of a contract in German held by the London head office of a UK firm. Electrical engineers working on a breakdown in a large machine at Dover may need to consult the manufacturer's original plan, held at their Bradford factory. A hospital in Hong Kong may require clinical notes relating to a patient who was last treated in Manchester. Needs can be met by a *facsimile transmission service*. The material, which can be up to A4 in size, is taken to a selected post-office, converted into digital form and sent to a receiving post-office where it appears as a black and white image. If the receiving office is in the UK, the papers can await collection, be delivered by special messenger or sent by first-class post. Coloured input will emerge as black and white output. This *Intelpost* system, as it is called, is available at certain main UK post-offices. Such transmission will be by landline, but even speedier means will use satellite or broadcast microwaves. Some users of the system own their own machine, *Fax*, and Intelpost operates to handle transmission to or from Fax. One advantage of facsimile transmission is that the sender keeps possession, once transmitted, of the original document.

Electronic post

The British Post Office provides a computerised service enabling a user to despatch batches of similar letters more speedily and cheaply than by conventional methods. Subscription reminders, quarterly reports and monthly price-lists sent out in large numbers by organisations and firms are suitable for the service, which operates from a main centre in London and several regional centres. The centre to be used keeps on computer file letter headings and signature for the user. The user provides, on a computer tape meeting Post Office requirements, the message to be posted, e.g. the body of a letter. The Post Office laser-prints the letters, folds them, inserts them in envelopes and seals them automatically, providing the stationery required.

Certain preprinted items provided by the user can be included. In the Standard Service, the letters are delivered at a time stated in the agreement made between the Post Office and the user. The Priority Service is more expensive, but if the material is at the centre by a stated time, the mail will leave the regional centre by first-class post the same day.

The services offer reproduction in a variety of type styles and arrangements for sending graphics. Confidentiality of the material posted is guarded by employing special staff, operating in lockable rooms and keeping the work separate from that of ordinary mail.

Telecom Gold

British Telecom Golden Electronic Mail provides an electronic mail service, which, once installed, is often more convenient to use than the conventional telephone, and the running costs are lower. All the subscribers have mail boxes electronically operated, each identified, like a telephone line, with a unique number.

The message is entered by keyboard, with the receiver's number and a statement of the subject of the message. Upon arrival, the subject is displayed on the receiver's screen, enabling the most urgent messages to be dealt with first while the rest can await attention. The system is safeguarded to protect confidentiality and, unlike some transmission methods, problems of incompatability between devices do not arise. The method can be used for communications between stations on one organisations's network and can also give cheap international access.

Electronic funds transfer

Strictly speaking, a book on information processing should not be concerned with the movement of anything else, so that the transfer of funds would be beyond the subject. The cliché that 'money talks' may be a superficial reason for discussing payment by computer here; the real reason is that funds can be moved electronically as simply and speedily as the record of the movement can be made.

The computerisation of bank internal and external transactions demonstrates this. A customer of a bank can obtain money in the form of notes by inserting a cash-card at a cash-point, and keying in his personal code. The local machine checks the identity number against the bank's central computer records and, if the customer's account is in credit, the computer signals the machine to release the money required. At one stroke, information about an account is updated and money is transferred. Other information-processing facilities offered at the cash-point are the ordering of a new cheque-book and the display of an account statement on the machine's screen. The customer's code is written in computer-readable form on a plastic strip on the customer's card.

In a newer system, the card has a fixed total withdrawal amount which is reduced by the amount of money withdrawn each time the card is used. A similar system is used in the new telephone-cards which allow call-boxes to be used without coins being inserted.

Credit-cards also allow funds to be transferred, and accounts debited, without coins changing hands.

In commercial banks, funds are transferred from one client's account to another's, or between bank and client, by the use of the bank's central and branch computers. At the same time, the accounts are processed. Magnetic ink recognition system (MICR) characters on cheques and paying-in slips indicate to the computer the document serial number, the branch and account number. At present, banks do not use methods by which a computer can read the amount of money; this is inserted, at processing, in MICR, thus enabling accounts to be debited and credited and particular cheques identified.

Where more than one bank is involved in settling a transaction, the cheque will go through the *Bankers' Automated Clearing System* in London. Once more, information will be updated on the account between two banks, and funds transferred without money changing hands.

The underlying method of recording and settling debts has now an international dimension with the operation of the *Society for World Interbank Financial Telecommunications (SWIFT)* from its Brussels headquarters.

At the present time a retailer accepting payment for goods and services with a credit-card has recovered payment by sending on to the credit card firm (e.g. Barclaycard, Access) a copy of the sales voucher signed by the customer at the time of the transaction.

A scheme recently announced by BP, electronic funds transfer at the point of sale (EFTPOS), is a further step towards the 'cashless society'. Machines have been installed at a large number of its petrol stations enabling customers with bank or building society cash-cards to pay for petrol from the till. The customer inserts his card and keys in his personal number, and his account is debited straight away. The company operating the scheme, Funds Transfer Sharing (FTS), includes two American banks, certain British building societies and other financial institutions.

Information recording and retrieval

In the running of any office, information will pass to and from the world outside, and will be recorded in the office itself. The oldest office systems used hand-writing and typing. The coming of electronics to the office brought greater changes in the kind of information, the method of storage and the devices used to handle it. An early example was the *teletypewriter* which would print slowly, character by character, information put into the computer. It could record output as well. It was slower than the VDU with which it was often associated. However, it provided a permanent, written record of information. Compared with more modern devices, it is comparatively cheap. It still has uses in logging main-frame performances, and lends itself to interactive work, as in the writing of computer programs, or in teaching subjects with computer aid, where rapid response to input is not essential.

Information useful to business organisations and individuals is becoming widely available through *videotex* systems. *Teletext* makes available, to people with ordinary TV screens and a set with this facility, general information about the weather, news, finance and other subjects. It is presented in numbered frames, an index is shown on the screen, and with a small electronic control the required frame can be selected. The BBC system is 'CEEFAX' and the IBA, 'ORACLE'. The arrangment is not interactive. The viewer must accept the information in predetermined form.

In *viewdata*, data reaches the user by a public telephone line and is displayed on a TV screen or VDU. *Prestel* is a scheme provided by British Telecom. A large amount of information is collected and made available to users. The pages required can be identified through a printed directory or an index displayed on the screen. To use the system, a number is dialled and a personal password entered. There is a charge for the service, and recent developments have extended the system to allow, under certain conditions, articles to be sold and paid for, telex messages to be sent and access to electronic mail to be obtained.

An organisation or business can provide its own *viewdata* system to communicate with members or customers. Access to such a system will be restricted by the user, and confidentiality will be maintained. Communication outside the user's premises can be by either public transmission or private line. The *Gateway* system gives a user the benefits of Prestel and his own private system.

Teleconferencing

In business life, the term 'conference' has described a face-to-face meeting of two or more people, e.g. in the same office or boardroom. With the development of telephone speech transmission a system of *teleconferencing* became possible enabling people in different places to confer continuously over a set period. Now that pictures and documents can be transmitted, the system has been enhanced so that each member of the conference can see the same document on his VDU while discussing it with his colleagues.

Electronic calendars and diaries

The introduction of electronics into offices can bring personal help to managers and others by reducing the work of listing names, addresses and telephone numbers, preparing calendars of events and writing up business diaries. Information of this kind can be kept on computer file for display on a VDU or for printing out as required. The use of codes can restrict full access so that, for example, an outside enquirer could discover when a conference room was free, or when an executive had no appointments, but complete information would be available only to the executive and his aides.

Further internal and external aspects of the electronic office

This chapter has described important machines found in the electronic office and has reviewed some of the simpler systems in which they are used. A comprehensive account of newer techniques would need to examine more closely a very large number of ways in which firms and organisations adopt the elements of the new technology to meet their special requirements, and there is no standard pattern which private networks follow. To make the account meaningful, some reference has been made to the work of the Post Office and British Telecom, but more needs to be said about their external transmission services, and those of Mercury Communications Ltd, and the next chapter will do this.

Short questions

1 Illustrate how the introduction of electronic devices and systems into an office could bring the following improvements:
 (a) saving in stationery;
 (b) speeding of work;
 (c) reduction in total human effort involved.

2 Suppose that you were the manager of a large office which used a number of electrical typewriters.
 (a) What arguments would you use to the firm when trying to replace them with word processors?
 (b) What arguments against the change might the firm put forward?

3 Explain why in some business systems word processors are used independently, whereas in others they are arranged to work in groups.

4 Give a realistic example of the substance of a telex message which you would expect to be handled by each of the following:
 (a) output by a teleprinter used by a British travel agent in relation to an overseas transaction;

130 Information Processing for Business Studies

(b) input to a teleprinter used by a large road haulage business operating in England, Wales and Scotland.

5   A London-based property developer has just received from his architect the site plans of a new estate which he is seeking permission to develop in Lancashire. Submission to the local council is urgent, if time is not to be lost through missing a meeting.

Explain how a facsimile transmission service could help him, outlining the procedure he would follow and mentioning any limitations of this method.

6   What are the main differences between sending mail electronically, when compared with the conventional system, for:
  (a) the sender;
  (b) the receiver;
  (c) the Post Office?

7   How would the following be likely to be involved in electronic funds transfer:
  (a) a main-frame computer;
  (b) another electronic device;
  (c) users of the service;
  (d) staffs of banks or similar institutions?

8   The introduction of electronic methods to business life has meant that on many occasions, and in different systems, the transmission of information has put pictures, diagrams, etc., on VDUs and TV screens. Draw up a varied list to illustrate this under the following headings (one example is given).

System	Firm or organisation using it	Picture, etc.
CEEFAX	Soft-fruit farmer	Weather report and forecast

9   During the past year a large office has changed from a manual system to a new one in which electronic devices and methods are used as much as possible. How would the following be affected by the changes:
  (a) the office manager;
  (b) typists who had used manual systems;
  (c) filing clerks?

Practical work

1   Find a local firm or organisation which uses one or more word processors. Give an account of their work including if possible information about:
  date of installation;
  reasons for installation;
  work done;
  special facilities which would not be given by an ordinary typewriter;

The electronic office and its setting **131**

whether the processor(s) work with another word processor, computer or other electronic device;
any problems encountered;
the user's general opinion on word processors.

2 Obtain from a post-office additional information about *either* facsimile transmission *or* electronic mail, including costs, speeds of delivery and conditions which users would need to observe.

Questions relevant to BTEC written examinations

1 (*a*) Describe the advantages which a word processor has over a typewriter.
(*b*) Explain one way in which a word processor can be used in a computer system.

2 (*a*) Explain briefly machines and systems available in the electronic office for the following kinds of work:
(*i*) despatching plans and documents;
(*ii*) keeping up to date on commodity and share prices;
(*iii*) holding conferences between senior managers with offices in separate places.
(*b*) How has the coming of the electronic office affected the work of ordinary office workers?

Other examination questions

1 Discuss the impact of information technology in the role of the office in the 1980s. (IAM – Administrative Management, Summer 1984)

2 Describe a computer-based system which can be used to facilitate 'paperless' transactions in shops and department stores. The system described should be able to provide:
(*a*) instant information on *each* customer's credit-worthiness;
(*b*) the means for settling an account on the spot, via the customer's bank.
(CGLI – Computer Programming and Information Processing, June 1985)

13 DATA TRANSMISSION TECHNIQUES AND SERVICES

> This chapter
> - explains the demand for new methods of data transmission;
> - describes the use of fibre optics;
> - describes the organisation of data-flows in transmission;
> - describes devices carrying more than one stream of data;
> - mentions microwave radio and satellite methods;
> - describes British Telecom public data network service, private circuit service, messaging services and services being developed;
> - describes Mercury Communications Ltd transmission system;
> - describes the Royal Mail Datapost service.

The modern demand

The coming of the electronic office described in the last chapter saw a number of new devices being used in data and information processing. At the same time, networks grew up within self-contained organisations, often linking to larger networks outside. New transmission techniques are needed to meet the new demand for quicker and more effective movement of data, in much larger quantities than before. In the UK the challenge is being met by both public and private sectors, and this chapter will touch on important changes in method and organisation that have occurred.

Telephone lines

A simple way of carrying an audible message between two distant points is to have a telephone at each end and a single insulated wire conveying an electric current between them. Such a system over any distance is rather inefficient. It is apt to suffer from both fading and distortion of the message and electrical interference from other telephone lines, not to mention other natural and manmade sources. Doubling the line and introducing other technical improvements produces a higher quality of performance reached by the public telephone service provided today in the UK. Such lines are extensively used for computer and associated electronic transmission, and examples have been given earlier. But the old lines are slow for their modern traffic, and new problems arise when they carry short bursts of electronic impulses instead of longer flows of continuous electric current.

Fibre-optic transmission

A very great advance in transmission methods has been made through the use of *fibre-optic* techniques. Instead of travelling as electronic impulses the succession of bits which make up a data message is carried as light in the form of laser beams. When a straight stick is partly immersed in water it appears to the observer to be bent and this property is used to prevent the laser beam escaping in transmission. It travels along a fibreglass core no wider than human hair, 'insulated' by a glass coating with a different refractive property. The method has a number of advantages. Transmission is very fast and the bandwidth is wide so that a range of frequencies can be carried, giving the channel great capacity. Connections are easily made. The material is small, so that lines can readily be run through cable conduits designed for the more cumbersome metal conductors. Because it is light, it can be suspended above ground and traverse mountainous country without the engineering problems associated with heavier cable, as experiments in telecommunication links in north and west Wales demonstrated a few years ago. Problems of interference from nearby lines or from natural causes do not arise, because light beams are used, and not electromagnetic impulses; for the same reason, underwater transmission is less prone to 'leakage' than electrically based systems.

A disadvantage of fibre-optic systems is that the signal weakens over a distance, and frequent *repeater stations* are needed. However, manufacturing techniques are improving, and better grades of fibreglass require fewer repeater stations. The most advanced uses very narrow-bore lines, with much more efficient performance, but certain manufacturing difficulties will need to be overcome before this grade becomes widely available.

Line organisation

Line systems are described according to their directional facilities, *simplex* carrying messages in only one direction, *duplex* in both directions simultaneously, and *half-duplex* in either direction, but not simultaneously.

134 Information Processing for Business Studies

In an ordinary telephone conversation, a message travels from the caller to his correspondent, and then another in the opposite direction, and so on, until one user replaces his telephone. Between the start and the finish, the line is in continuous use. Where messages are depersonalised, the substance can be sub-divided, stored temporarily if need be, and the packets into which they have been broken can be reassembled at output so that

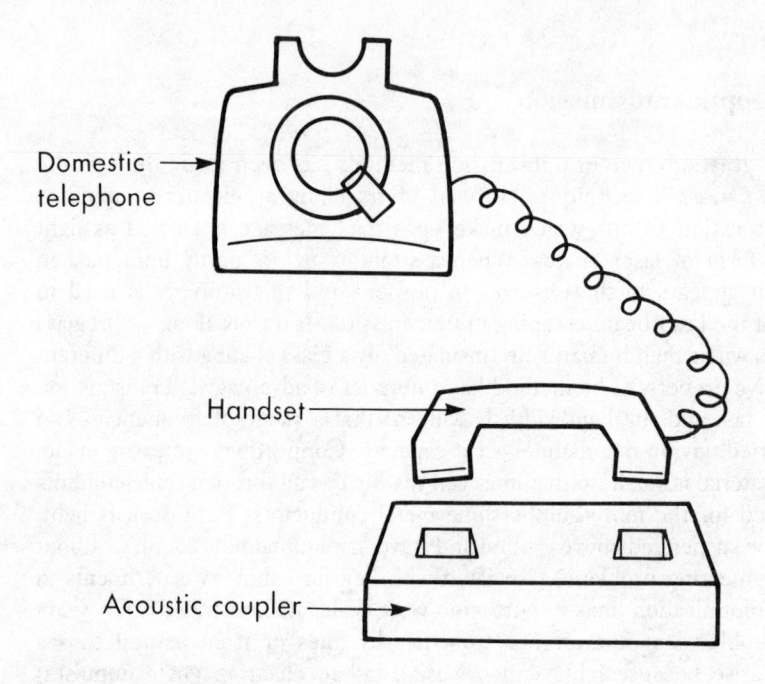

Fig. 13.1 Acoustic coupler

the messages are received in their original form. This method is called *packet switching* and enables the best use to be made of a line, a number of messages being transmitted at once, and gaps in the use of the line being minimised. A public service example is given later in this chapter.

A cheaper device that serves the same purpose as a *modem*, described in Chapter 12, is the *acoustic coupler*. The simplest type is portable, interfacing with a terminal and fitting on to an ordinary telephone handset, and converting data received into a form suitable for transmission along the telephone wire. A corresponding coupler fitted to the telephone at the other end transforms the data for terminal output. Alternatively the system works through couplers built into the terminal. Modems are quicker than couplers in transmission.

Multiple access

In modern computing, a number of terminals will be connected to one computer and a system of input and output traffic control will be needed. One method is to employ a special mini- or microcomputer, a front-end processor, to do this, as explained in Chapter 7.

An early device used to meet the problem was called a *concentrator*. This was a buffering device, accepting bits from the various terminals, and despatching them at high speed to the computer. Where terminals are conveniently grouped together, *multiplexing* may be practised. A *multiplexer* organises the input of bits from the terminals into suitable patterns for the computer. Where a wide waveband line is used, the system can be made more effective through two or more waves being used at the same time.

Other communication methods

Transmission through space is quicker and, over long distances, cheaper than along pre-laid material lines. Two main systems acknowledge this. In *microwave radio* systems, messages are conveyed by short-wave radio between pairs of dishes facing one another at heights great enough to clear intervening objects. The other system uses *satellites* in *geostationary orbits*, i.e. in paths which always keep them over the same positions on the earth's surface. They must be placed more than 20 miles above and be moving in relation to the atmosphere at high speeds. Messages are beamed from a fixed earth station on to a satellite, across to another satellite and down to the receiving station.

British Telecom – Public Data Network Services

Most of the developments of the electronic office described in the last chapter will use external means of communication in common with businesses, organisations and members of the public, and British Telecom's Public Data Network offers three main types of service of this kind. *Packet switch stream (PSS)* carries electronic mail, enables terminals to retrieve information from a central computer, links point-of-sale devices to their host's computer, and provides the main ways in which companies through computing can transact financial and other business between one another. A specialised service, *Mediat*, provides communications for the insurance industry and links insurance companies to brokers. The *closed user group (CUG)* facility provides some of the advantages of a private network, allowing users of it to communicate with one another but excluding other calls to and from the group. The *multistream* service enlarges the scope of the PSS scheme through *multistream access points* which are being increasingly provided. It is possible to reach most of the users through the telephone by local-rate calls, and for others through *protocols*, special instructions required, in this case, to ensure the proper transmission of a packet of data. The third service, *international packet switch stream*, enables a PSS customer to extend his available network to more than 50 overseas data networks.

British Telecom private circuit services

Paying an annual rent for the exclusive use of a private line offers various advantages: dialling is reduced; access to another user is fast and direct; and the scheme can be customised to the user's requirements. Generally, charges are not made for calls, so that if the volume of traffic is high the method is economical. The *Speechline* service is designed mainly for speech transmission, whereas *Keyline* handles data as well. Where a large number of channels are to be served, for voice and data the most economical method is to use the *wideband private circuit* system.

These three services are analogue in principle. Private line digital transmission is provided by two services. *Kilostream* carries data and voice at varying high-speed rates, with a 24-hour maintenance service. It is suitable for bulk data transfer, facsimile work and video conferencing. Higher speeds still are possible through the *Mega stream* service, and it can support large networks. A firm with a number of different sites, or using *computer aided design (CAD)* or *computer aided manufacture (CAM)*, would find it valuable.

British Telecom messaging services

These include the *telex network*, supporting systems of telex machines in their most modern form, as described in Chapter 12. The corporation sells telex terminals, and is modernising the network through the provision of *stored program control (SPC)* techniques at new exchanges.

The *Teletext* service transmits documents between terminals such as word processors and electronic typewriters, access being obtained through the telephone system or PSS. An A4 page of text can be sent from one end of the country to the other in 20 seconds at a low cost.

The remaining messaging service, *Telecom Gold*, was mentioned in Chapter 12. It is backed by a 24-hour *Helpline* service, and it is connected to 13 other countries. Users can take advantage of a CUG facility.

Services being developed by British Telecom

Accounts given so far of British Telecom services show an evolution from the original telephonic system to a series of communicating networks with associated devices, with old and slow methods giving way to efficient, fast and modern schemes for carrying messages by voice, by document, by picture and by printed text between points in the UK and beyond. The aim is to set up an overland scheme, *Integrated Services Digital Network*, giving the advantages of a unified and completely digitised system, to be accessed through *integrated digital access (IDA)*. An *IDA pilot* service based on large digital exchanges in London, Birmingham and Manchester has already started, and performances in some of the services already described have improved.

Cable-distributed communication is being developed, enabling the range of TV programmes available to viewers to be increased through a satellite which feeds a computerised distribution point. Cable transmission is also being used for interactive services such as tele-banking, home security and video libraries. Contact is made in the home from a new type of TV receiver.

Additional facilities for transmitting entertainment, business information and local broadcasting are being developed through satellites and small-dish earth terminals, within the UK.

Another new feature of British Telecom is its message handling service (MHS), where messages are delivered as documents in envelopes to the receiver. Access will be in a variety of ways, such as telex, and an electronic directory of users is available. Between parties on the Telecom network, urgent delivery can occur within ten minutes. Normal delivery is within two hours and non-urgent within eight hours.

Mercury Communications Ltd

In 1984 the BT monopoly of telecommunications systems in the UK was ended by law and substantial competition was introduced when Mercury Communications Ltd, a member of Cable and Wireless Worldwide Communications Group, was fully licensed by the Department of Industry. In the UK, they operate through a modern transmission system, shown in Fig. 13.2. Trunk optical fibre cables stretch in a rough triangle with its base from Exeter to Brighton, via Southampton, and an apex at Birmingham, enabling London, Bristol and some other large towns to be served; an additional cable links Bristol directly to London. From Birmingham a loop takes in Manchester, Leeds and Nottingham. Trunk microwave systems link this network to Cardiff and Swansea, and Glasgow, Dundee, Aberdeen and Edinburgh, with a short line to Chelmsford. In a few places straight trunk microwave lines provide shorter alternative connections between places on the cable system.

Access to the trunk network is obtained through the places mentioned and other distribution nodes by fibre optic cable in the area served. Branches up to 25 km in length are served by 2 Mb/s radio links and by 64 kb/s

138 Information Processing for Business Studies

for 10 km. More distant places are usually reached by microwave radio relay. The trunk circuits are laid in loops, with signals travelling both ways round each loop, and if a fault occurs the device at output will automatically turn the flow on to the sound circuit. Other characteristics claimed for Mercury transmission are high-quality voice output and speeds more than three times

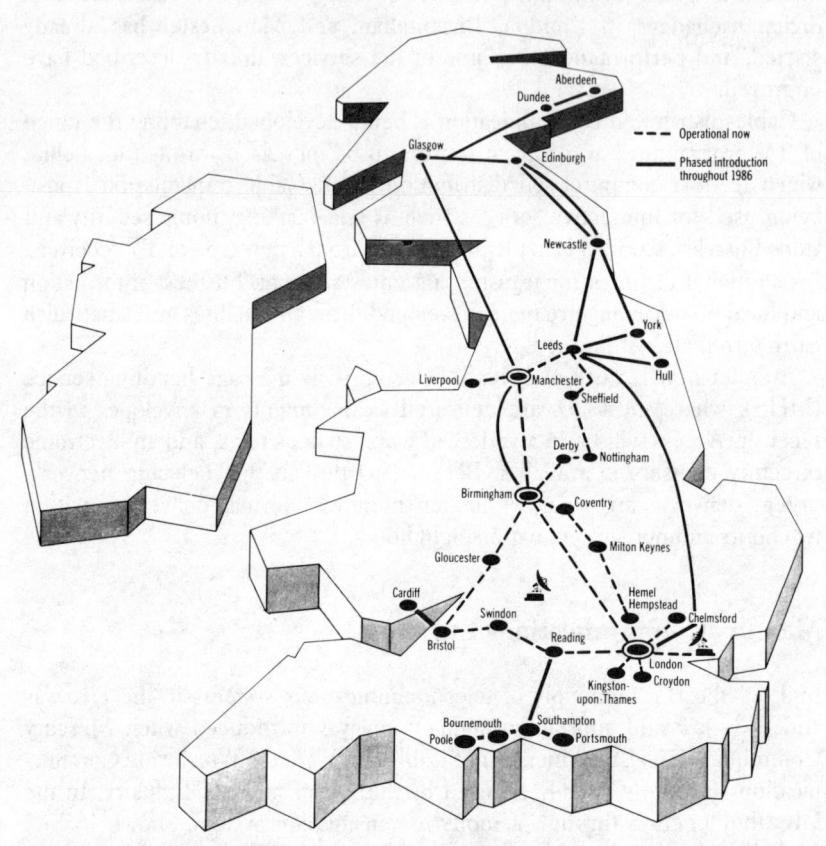

Fig. 13.2 Network of transmission lines in the UK (*by courtesy of Mercury Communications Ltd*)

those of older systems. A 24-hour maintenance system throughout the year is guaranteed, and the standard time for an engineer to reach a site is four hours. A special *effective management communication* programme has been designed to give good service to customers. Customers will find transmission suitable for a wide range of requirements, including video conferencing, facsimile despatch and high-quality TV broadcasts.

Mercury has five satellite communication stations at present on two sites, Whitehall and Dockland Developments and plans to include satellite links to the Caribbean, the Middle East and to offshore structures. A new market-link transatlantic optical fibre cable is planned to come into service in the UK in 1989.

In 1986, Mercury introduced the first alternative national telephone scheme, which is available to large businesses – examples of customers being the Midland Bank and Grand Metropolitan. Later in the year the alternative system will be available to small businesses and to residential customers. Considerable savings on both international and UK services are claimed.

Royal Mail Services

In 1970, the Post Office started Datapost, a courier service mainly to meet the demand of a growing computer industry for quick delivery of data,

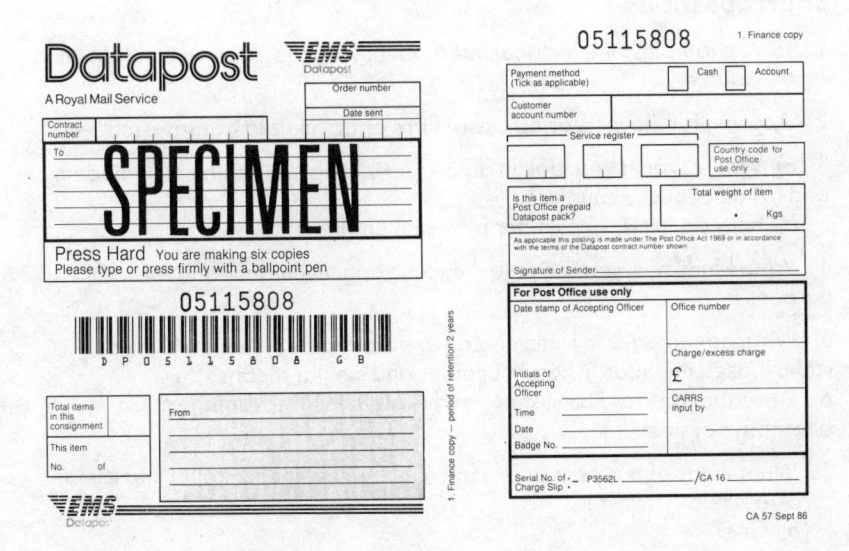

Fig. 13.3 *(by courtesy of the Post Office)*

programs, etc., by physical means, as distinct from electronic transmission. Soon, the demand stretched beyond computer related traffic to include more general commercial material. The name is unchanged, and a great deal of data is still carried. It can be engaged through a Freefone service, and operates through Datapost service centres, through a large number of post offices carrying the Datapost sign and through postal representatives.

In the overnight service, the item will generally be delivered by noon the next day. Each item is subject to a weight limit, but the total weight of a consignment is unlimited. *International Datapost* is a timetabled service which takes packages abroad to any of 56 countries. Size and weight limits depend upon the country of destination. Packages receive priority in customs clearance. A long journey, e.g. from Birmingham to Tokyo, will take only three days, and shorter journeys will take less. The Datapost Sameday service works through Datapost service centres, guaranteeing collection and delivery in one day, with a money-back guarantee. An item, but not a consignment, must meet a maximum weight limit.

Where use of Datapost is likely to be regular, contracts can be arranged. High volume users may gain a discount and obtain free regular collections. Contract users may buy from the Post Office padded containers for their packages.

Royal Mail services provide customers with free insurance for both inland and overseas packages. In the event of non-delivery, settlements are claimed to be very generous for direct and consequential losses.

Short questions

1. Give examples of 'electrical interference' from (a) 'natural' and (b) 'man-made' sources.

2. Account for the increasing use of fibre optics in data transmission.

3. (a) Where would you look in data-transmitting systems for (i) a modem and (ii) an acoustic coupler?
   (b) How do the devices differ from one another?

4. What kinds of systems employ multiplexing techniques and for what purpose?

5. What advantages in transmission are offered by systems which use radio-based methods instead of cables and similar means?

6. Describe uses for PSS systems and explain their advantage over alternative systems.

7. What kinds of business or organisation would find the following useful:
   (a) bulk data transfer;
   (b) CAD;
   (c) CAM?

8. Give examples of British Telecom services using the following techniques:
   (a) digital transmission;
   (b) satellites;
   (c) personal delivery.
Name for each a business or organisation that would find the service useful.

9. Express in your own words three important points which a Mercury Communications sales representative might make in trying to persuade a large business to use their services.

10. A firm which uses a computer bureau some miles from its premises for data and information processing wishes to send each week batches of source documents and to receive back as soon as possible the documents

Data transmission techniques and services 141

and print-outs prepared from them. Describe how the Post Office could help, and explain important points which would need to be settled between both parties before the firm used the service.

Practical work

1 By enquiries at the local British Telecom office obtain leaflets and booklets relating to the Merlin line of products which they sell.

(a) List the products, adding brief notes about the general purpose which each serves.

(b) Select one of the products which appears to relate to a service mentioned in one of the last two chapters. Write brief notes about its design, facilities and performance. (*Note:* Some of the information is highly technical, and you would not be expected to have a complete understanding of all of it.)

2 (a) Collect information about Datapost facilities available to an intended user in your district. Include reference to:

(i) addresses of premises from which they are operated;

(ii) some idea of the actual facilities and cost on the basis of imaginary loads (e.g. 2-kg parcels three times weekly, on specified days for delivery at a named town about 100 miles away).

(b) Collect information about services and costs for the same packages using the ordinary mail or parcel services.

(c) Write a few notes on conclusions you have reached about the two methods.

Questions relevant to BTEC written examinations

1 (a) State briefly different modern methods by which data can travel between firms and organisations.

(b) Select one of these methods, describe the terminals and explain with reasons why the method would meet a particular kind of need.

2 Give an account of a modern data-transmission system provided by each of the following:
  (a) British Telecom (do not include the ordinary telephone service);
  (b) The Royal Mail (do not include the domestic delivery service);
  (c) Mercury Communications Ltd.

Other examination questions

1 What equipment, other than telephones, is available to assist the communications function within an organisation? (IAM – Certificate, Methods and Systems, Winter 1985)

2 Write short notes on any two of the following:
  (a) electronic mail;
  (b) microfilm storage media;
  (c) public data networks.
(IAM – Certificate, Methods and Systems, Winter 1984)

14 INTRODUCING COMPUTER SYSTEMS TO ORGANISATIONS

This chapter
- explains the main reasons why businesses and other organisations introduce new computer-based systems and extend existing ones;
- describes the main steps – initial investigation, feasibility study, applying systems analysis, system design and implementation;
- mentions the part played by organisation and method techniques, systems specification, and the steering committee.

Introducing and extending computer systems into businesses and other organisations

Foregoing chapters have in broad outline described what computer-based systems are and how they are used to provide data and information for the organisations served. This chapter will describe the main stages by which organisations decide to introduce systems and implement their decisions; and some of these stages will be followed where major changes in existing systems are discussed and then carried out. These general procedures usually involve the drawing of charts and the writing and testing of programs, to be explained in Chapter 15.

The term 'computer system' is used advisedly, as the outcome of proposals may not be the installation of an in-house computer, but the provision of computing facilities entirely through a computer bureau. In a few cases, the circumstances which prompted the idea of computerisation may have so altered, or the necessary expenditure may be so high, that the proposals have to be abandoned; but the post-natal mortality rate in computer schemes is comparatively low.

The mainstream of ideas that flood into a computer installation or extension may be fed in a variety of ways. A business which sees a rival using computer systems which it does not possess may, as a matter of prestige, wish to keep up with it; or, more sensibly, it may argue that unless it modernises, it may be unable to face competition in the field. Advertising pressure from firms selling computers and software will have some effect, particularly with smaller firms. A firm large enough to have its own computer department will have a potential inbuilt spring from which ideas for expansions will overflow, for systems development is likely to be one of its permanent terms of reference. Probably the commonest incentive to look into the possibilities of computerisation is the existence of an urgent problem, such as the rising cost of manual clerical processes or a growing inability to process and execute orders from stock to time, for which a new system is the only answer.

The initial installation of a major computer system, with the costs of hardware, software and specialised staff, is a major capital venture, and unless successful, it can have serious and perhaps irreversible consequences for the firm. Readers may recall from Chapter 3 that business planning covered varying spans of time and operated at related levels in an organisation. A major installation would be a matter for *corporate planning*. This provides a scheme which determines the policies of all the firm's departments over a period of time, at least four and often five years. Included would be subordinate plans for raising the capital, acquiring equipment, altering the buildings, adjusting the personnel structure and re-organising the input and output of documents. Aspects of the scheme would be detailed timetables, departmental budgets and manpower allocations. The final objective would be a proven computer system in full and effective operation.

A small, one-man business may become computerised more quickly and with less formality. The businessman may purchase outright or lease a microcomputer with a minimum of peripherals. Software may come with the machine, and the manufacturer may supply stationery for such systems as billing or pay-roll. The signing of a service agreement may be the only formal step in a transaction which, despite its informality, is of a kind which is working well with hundreds of small businesses in the UK today.

Initial investigation

The introduction of the small system mentioned in the last paragraph probably occurred with the minimum of preliminaries. The businessman probably approached the manufacturer directly with a brief statement of his problem or what he considered to be his needs. The manufacturer's representative would visit him and make a brief survey of the existing system, and the businessman would receive a free estimate of a system or alternative systems. He would then decide whether or not to go ahead. Although such arrangements are simple, they make the user rather dependent on one source, both in initial choice of equipment, software and system, and afterwards in maintenance and possible expansion, where considerations of compatibility may constrict future development. Obtaining the services of a computer consultant will make his decisions freer and better informed; but consultancy is usually associated with large enterprises. Moreover, it is apt to be expensive for the small man, and an estimate of the costs involved should be obtained beforehand.

In market research, before a large project is commissioned, a firm may engage a management consultant to report whether the project is needed at all. A firm's sales difficulties may arise from causes which an ordinary market research project would not reveal such as stealing by stockroom staff, incompetence of the sales director or an outdated management structure. The report is called a *situation analysis*, and an objective survey of this kind might save the expense of a *feasibility survey*, which is the next step usually taken by a firm seeking the extension or the first-time application of a computer system.

Feasibility study

Before a major enterprise is launched, such as the installation of a mainframe computer and the associated systems, two major decisions must be made by management: the first is concerned with whether the proposal is justified, and if so, what its general shape will be, and the information needed for a decision will come from a *feasibility study*. If as a result the project is approved, a larger, longer and more detailed investigation, known as a *systems analysis*, must be carried out, after which other stages will follow until the new system is completed and working satisfactorily.

The feasibility of the scheme will depend upon technical factors which will determine whether the problem can be solved or the proposed developments will work, upon the ability of the old organisation to be reshaped to take the new system, and most importantly of all upon whether it will be cost-effective.

The crucial decisions at this first stage are likely to be the concern of upper and middle management. Ideally, a small, skilled team should study the proposals and produce in broad outline a report for the board. For an extension of existing computing facilities, the organisation will presumably have its own department or professional staff to guide it. The finance director will clearly need to be heard, and departmental heads immediately concerned must be brought in. For example, a large manufacturing firm which proposed to computerise its commercial procedures as a first step, leaving manufacturing to a later stage, would probably put its accountant and sales manager on the team, but not its works manager or engineer. It would be well advised to keep union representatives informed of the feasibility study, with more active participation being offered at the next stage, once the principle of a scheme has been approved.

Organisation and methods (O&M)

Before computers were introduced into business life, techniques and staff had developed in firms and other organisations for studying the way in which systems worked with a view to improving the quality of output, reducing staff and lowering running costs. The organisational side of the techniques studied the structure of the body in question, for example the *span of control* in a department, i.e. the number of subordinates who could be effectively controlled by a superior, or the relationship of a local council's finance committee to its departmental committees, such as highways or library. The methods side was concerned with activities, such as the internal distribution, collection and despatch of mail in a large administrative department. Most methods studies related to clerical work, but some tackled activities which had little to do with paperwork, such as the use of both human effort and mechanical sweepers in street cleaning. When computers became available, the O&M department could report that the best answer to a particular problem was the establishment of a computer.

Presently, as the possibilities of computerisation dominated the business scene, systems investigation became the responsibility of new and separate departments. Today, an organisation may be large enough to sustain organised groups of people practising O&M and systems analysis, which is the next step to be described. In a large hospital, for example, a study in 'O' might be concerned with the working relationships between medical staff and administration, 'M' might investigate the loading and routeing of instrument trolleys which nurses wheel to patients' bedsides, and a systems analysis project could aim for a better system for filing and retrieving medical data. Whatever the arrangements made, or the titles given to the investigation groups, systems analysis techniques have much in common with those developed in earlier days when O&M was introduced.

Analytical techniques

Although the feasibility study may have shown the need for a new system, or the extension of an existing one, a closer and more technical analysis will be required before the changes can be made. Generally, the analysis will be the first stage in a sequence called the *systems life cycle*, and will be followed by design of the new system, its implementation and maintenance, with periodical review and the prospect in a rapidly changing technology of a full-circle return to the analysis stage.

Analysis begins with a full and impartial study of all the facts, and where possible their verification, the output being in the form of charts and diagrams, written reports and sometimes tape-recordings. A variety of charts and diagrams may be needed. From them will be written the programs to be used in the new system, and they will be described in Chapter 14.

The total information collected will describe what is being done, who is doing it, how they are doing it, and the place of particular activities in the whole sequence. Where appropriate, the accounts will be quantitative, mentioning such facts as the number of copies of documents, times and frequencies (for example of using machines), and the dimensions of forms. Reports may also include the analyst's judgments, e.g. that inaccuracies in office output were due to inadequate training or staffing levels, or that some forms of stationery could be improved. The main ways of collecting facts are by interviewing, observing, issuing questionnaires and reading records. Collection should generally start at the highest level, with top management, and proceed systematically to the lowest, with permission always being obtained from the level above that at which investigation is being made. The information sought will relate to the level, with top management being concerned with policies and broad strategies, and middle management being able to throw light on major departmental issues; at levels below, where most of the enquiries are likely to occur, the investigation will cover the details of daily working routines.

Interviews are ideally conducted in a relaxed atmosphere in private. The analyst should know in general the areas to be explored. He should be objective, avoid as far as possible expressing opinions, and gently steer the respondent away from irrelevancies. Tape-recorders are sometimes used, and are effective provided that tension is not created in the respondent. They would be suitable for long interviews where discussion was likely to be open-ended. Where information is likely to be narrower, more concrete and readily classified, then brief notes can be made at interview, and perhaps general impressions written up afterwards. Interviewing may be impracticable where the views of a large number of respondents are being sought, or where they are scattered over a wide area. Required information may be obtained by sending to members of staff a questionnaire, with an explanatory covering letter, and arranging for collection or return by a specified day. The replies may be less accurate than with interviews, as misunderstandings are more likely to occur, and are more difficult to discover and rectify. Unless the employer compels the staff to return the questionnaires a number may not be returned. Replies obtained under duress, however, are unlikely to be as reliable as those freely made. Where numbers are very large, random sampling may be used, and the range of error statistically calculated.

Given sufficient time, facts can be collected by observation as a main method, or to supplement one of the other methods. Times taken over processes can be measured and recorded, numbers of documents can be counted, and the pattern of activities can be studied in a general way. A problem to be overcome is that the presence of an observer is likely to create a situation which is not normal, until the observer is accepted and his presence ignored.

Records and similar documents can sometimes reveal facts which are useful to a study of a situation. An obvious example would be an earlier report on the system; another would be an account of an auditor's investigation into a problem.

Where possible, facts should be verified. For example, in a study of a stock-keeping system, an analyst may enquire of the stores manager about the rules, documents and activities relating to the issue of stock. Quite independently he could collect facts about the transaction from someone drawing stock from the stores. Comparing the two accounts of the same transaction may reveal inconsistencies which can only be removed by further enquiries of each side.

Scope of survey

The contents of the report made at this stage will obviously depend upon the systems being studied, but most of the following points are likely to be covered. The objectives of the systems will be stated but, in systems which have evolved or have been built up piecemeal, precise objectives may be difficult to define. Inputs will be described and their form, their points of access, their volume and their frequency will be mentioned. Similar headings will be used in describing outputs. Staff directly involved, with their grades and individual responsibilities, will be described under the headings of input processing, output and supervision. Systems will not operate in complete freedom, and a proper account of existing procedure will need to mention environmental working standards laid down by law, union agreements as they affect working practices and the practical limitations imposed by the building and site. To lead naturally to the next stage, the report will reach a conclusion about the problem, or the possibility of development, which it was commissioned to discover.

System design

Once the case for a new or an amended system has been established, then it must be designed. Whereas in earlier accounts and discussions the forward input – processing – output sequence has been followed, the logical starting point for design is at output, as this will determine what goes before in the new system. In computerising a pay-roll system, for example, the contents of the pay-slip which goes to each worker must be decided, together with its layout and its relationship to the complete statement, the weekly pay-roll. A good system will take into account present or future need for management information in aid of decision making; in this example, an analysis of overtime or the effect of wage payments on cash-flow, to suggest two possibilities, can be produced. Where the new system extends or alters an existing one, changes in hardware and software must be considered, and perhaps some new equipment will be needed. For an entirely manual system, much work will be needed to choose a new computer and peripherals. In either case, new forms of input will have to be designed, which will mean changes in documents, procedures and sometimes in staff responsibilities and numbers. The new design will provide all the data and information required with economy of cost, manpower and time. It will meet standards of security and privacy, and take into account requirements of the Data Protection Act, to be described in Chapter 16. A good system will anticipate future expansion, and will minimise problems of compatibility.

Implementation

Once the system design has been approved, it will be implemented. If the old system was entirely manual, hardware must be acquired. The usual procedure is for specifications of the various devices to be drawn up, then tenders to be invited, considered by management and accepted or rejected. The hardware contract may cover software provided by the computer manufacturer. Most installations will require other software, and this can be bought-in or leased from outside, or written by the user's own programmers.

Staff will be much affected by implementation. Some may be made redundant or transferred to other work outside the computer and processing systems. A new team of computer professionals may need to be appointed. Two types of training courses may be needed, the first for staff directly engaged in preparing data and processing and the second for those whose work will be affected by the new system, and for whom a *computer appreciation course* would be helpful.

The new system may be introduced in various ways. The old system may be closed down entirely, after which the new system may take over. A small firm, for example, could use a weekend between two working weeks for the transition. Experience would suggest that any large system needs a little time to settle down, for it is almost impossible to foresee all the problems which may arise. In *parallel running* the old and new systems overlap in time, the new taking only some of the input until the user can be confident that the new system can take the full load. In *pilot running*, old data already processed is put into the new system. When comparison shows that the new output is sound, the old system is abandoned. When the changeover is *phased*, the two systems are run in parallel, but at first only a small proportion of the total input, e.g. stock records relating to one product, are fed into the new. Provided that the outcome is satisfactory, the input is increased until the full load is taken up.

In a large system, an essential stage will be maintenance to ensure that it is working satisfactorily and to forestall breakdowns. Computers and peripherals will receive the regular maintenance provided for any machine. In addition, test programs will be run to check the individual parts of the system, and the system as a whole. Regular assessment of performance may occur, and periodical review will be directed to updating the system in the light of changing conditions.

Systems specification

Before a new system is implemented, the management must give its formal approval to the proposals regarding input, processing and output, the acquiring of software and hardware. Staff changes and the method of implementation are set out in some detail in a *systems specification*.

Administering investigation and change

The arrangements which a particular organisation makes for initiating, controlling and completing the changes from a manual to a computer-based system will vary with the organisation, the scale of the enterprise and other factors such as whether consultants are engaged and whether the organisation has any technical staff. For changes of any magnitude, a powerful parent body, usually called a *steering committee*, is set up representing the board of directors or equivalent interests in non-commercial undertakings such as local councils, heads of departments and technical staff. It will appoint the small group undertaking the feasibility study. Systems investigation on a large scale will use small investigation teams, with each probably under the leadership of a senior systems analyst and including representatives of the department being studied. The steering committeee will co-ordinate the work of investigating teams, control budgets and timetables and choose tenders for hardware and software. It will oversee implementation, dealing with problems which may arise.

Short questions

1 The idea of installing an information-processing system for the first time in a firm or organisation may come from a number of possible sources. Explain them, stating with reasons the relative weight which you would give to each source.

2 A small one-man business is under considerable sales pressure to install a microcomputer-based system, but the proprietor is not yet convinced that he needs one. Draft *four* probing questions which he could put to the manufacturer's representative (do not mention purchase price) and suggest the lines of the replies.

3   Why are feasibility studies necessary?

4   Why is it desirable to keep trade unions informed of proposals to install computing systems?

5   Select some part of the clerical processes you would expect to find in the head office of a mail order firm at present operating on manual systems. Explain the ways in which a systems analyst might investigate the processes.

6   A systems analyst is *observing* the issuing of stocks of raw materials and components to be used in the construction of articles in an engineering firm. What is he likely to be looking for, and why?

7   A multiple-shop system wishes to computerise the paperwork which passes between its head office and its branches. It is inconvenient for the systems analyst to visit the branches and information is to be collected by postal questionnaire. State the main subjects you would expect to be covered by the questionnaire.

8   Explain in a few sentences why it is desirable for thorough investigations to be made before a large new computer system is installed.

9   (a) Explain briefly what is meant by 'systems design'.
   (b) If the term referred to proposed changes at the head office of a national society with paid members throughout the UK, how would the following be concerned:
   (i) stationery;
   (ii) staff?

10   State the different kinds of people you would expect to find on a steering committee, and justify their inclusion.

Practical work

1   Obtain permission to study a simple set of clerical procedures in a non-computerised setting, e.g. payment of accounts over an office counter, reception of cars for a regular service at a garage, the issue of student's union membership cards, etc. Simulate the work of a systems analyst by
   (a) noting and describing the procedures;
   (b) describing how documents are involved;
   (c) preparing and putting questions to those involved;
   (d) suggesting ways of verifying the facts collected.
State general impressions you have gathered from the exercise.

2   Choose either an organisation to which you have access which is on a manual system, or an imaginary one from the following list.
   (a) A farmers' co-operative society which buys raw materials and sells them at discount to members, hires out agricultural equipment, markets produce collectively and offers advice.
   (b) A local society which organises voluntary workers into such social work as visiting the aged, providing help in cases of poverty and providing holidays for the disabled.

(c) A taxi and car-hire firm.

Explain the stages by which the organisation changed from a manual system to a computer-centred one, giving some illustrative detail referring to the particular organisation you have chosen. Set out briefly the benefits to be expected from the change.

Questions relevant to BTEC written examinations

1 Give a reasoned account of the main stages by which a manual office system would be converted to a computerised one.

2 (a) Describe the methods by which a systems analyst can obtain information about the system he is studying.

(b) What can he do to encourage the co-operation of the people who will be providing information?

Other examination questions

1 Effective implementation is crucial to the success of new computer systems. Outline the aspects of implementation for which the systems analyst would plan. (CIPFA – Professional Examination 1, Systems Theory and Data Processing paper, Nov. 1984)

2 (a) Computers can be purchased, rented or leased from manufacturers. What advantages are to be gained where the computer is purchased?

(b) What does a Computer feasibility study seek to establish and indicate?
(A long rambling answer is not required – give five sound reasons which should be clearly and concisely explained.) (AAT – Data Processing, June 1982)

3 An existing manual system has to be implemented on a computer.

(a) Identify the various stages through which the computer project should pass.

(b) Suggest ways in which information can be obtained about the existing system.

(c) Describe two techniques by which changeover from the existing manual system to the new computer system might be achieved. (RSA – June 1984)

15 CHARTS, DIAGRAMS AND SOFTWARE FOR SIMPLE PROJECTS

> This chapter
> - describes charts and programs used in introducing a computer-based system, including organisation charts, block diagrams, systems flow charts, and simple programs in BASIC;
> - explains conditional statements, branches and loops, rounding, decision tables and choice of programming languages.

Completing a simple project

Chapter 14 drew the main outlines of the stages followed in introducing or extending a computer-based system. To complete the account, much detailed technical work is needed, and this will be done mainly by systems analysts and programmers. This chapter will describe separately the most important items in either graphic, coded or written form and then integrate them into the completion of a simple system.

Organisation charts

The simplest form of organisation chart sets out people or departments vertically at different levels and includes relationships between the parts concerned. Each unit is usually 'boxed' in a rectangle as shown in Fig. 15.1. Sometimes the rectangle gives additional information about the unit, one scheme being shown in Fig. 15.2.

An organisation chart shows at a glance the relative positions of the units, various levels of management staff, and the main channels of communication. A complete plan of all lines of communication would be complicated: obviously in this firm the production manager and marketing manager will be in horizontal touch over matters of product design, and copies of order forms and invoices will pass diagonally between the accountant and the purchasing officer.

Other applications of organisation charts are to show the relationship between a company and its subsidiaries, or the internal organisation of a

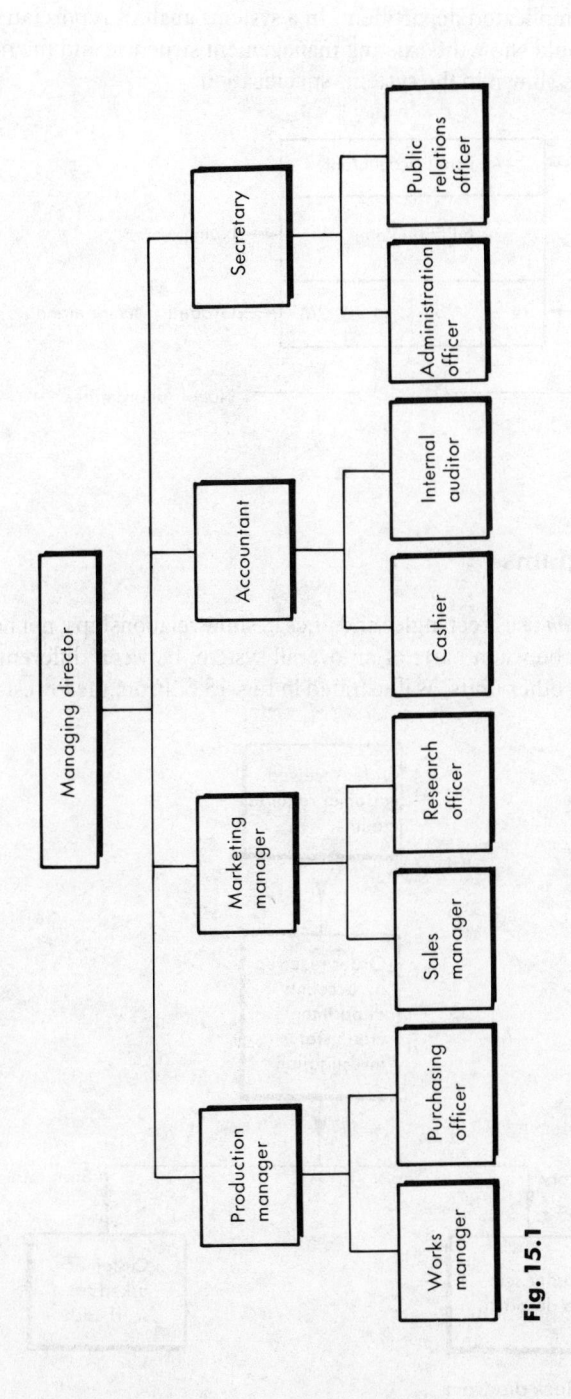

Charts, diagrams and software for simple projects **153**

```
                        ┌─────────────────┐
                        │Managing director│
                        └────────┬────────┘
        ┌───────────────┬────────┼────────┬───────────────┐
┌───────┴───────┐ ┌─────┴─────┐ ┌┴────────┐ ┌────────┐
│Production     │ │Marketing  │ │Accountant│ │Secretary│
│manager        │ │manager    │ │          │ │         │
└───┬───────┬───┘ └──┬─────┬──┘ └──┬────┬──┘ └──┬───┬──┘
    │       │        │     │       │    │       │   │
┌───┴──┐ ┌──┴───┐ ┌──┴──┐ ┌┴────┐ ┌┴───┐ ┌┴────┐ ┌─┴──┐ ┌┴──────┐
│Works │ │Purch.│ │Sales│ │Res. │ │Cash│ │Int. │ │Adm.│ │Public │
│mgr.  │ │off.  │ │mgr. │ │off. │ │ier │ │audit│ │off.│ │rel.off│
└──────┘ └──────┘ └─────┘ └─────┘ └────┘ └─────┘ └────┘ └───────┘
```

Fig. 15.1

large and complicated department. In a systems analysis report, an organisation chart could show the existing management structure and the new structure could be shown in the systems specification.

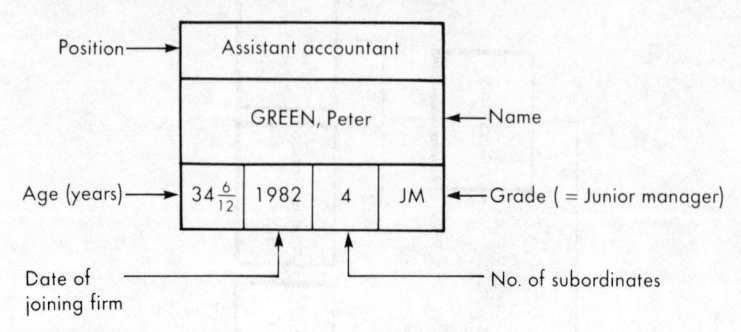

Fig. 15.2

Block diagrams

A *block diagram* uses rectangles and lines to show relationships, not necessarily hierarchical, between parts of an overall system, between different systems, and between other units, as illustrated in Fig. 15.3. From the lowest left-hand

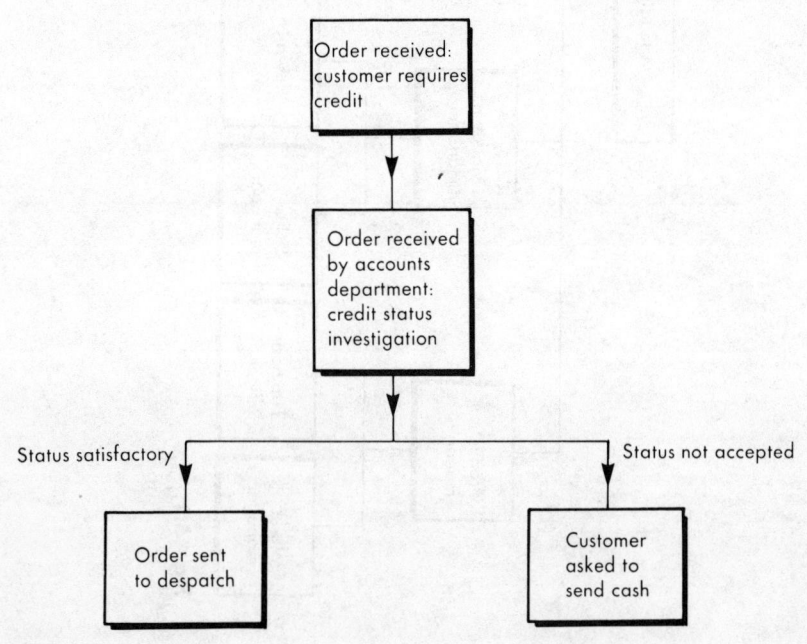

Fig. 15.3 Block diagram

rectangle in this figure another block diagram could be developed showing the raising of an invoice, the distribution of copies and the movement of other documents in the completion of the purchase. The second and third tiers are linked by a conditional decision, which in the next type of diagram to be described would be more clearly shown by a special symbol.

Flowcharts

An essential stage in the writing of all but the simplest computer programs is the drawing of more than one flowchart. A flowchart describes the sequence of events and the flow of information and documents in a business or other organisation, using lines and a code of symbols. Those shown in Figs 15.4

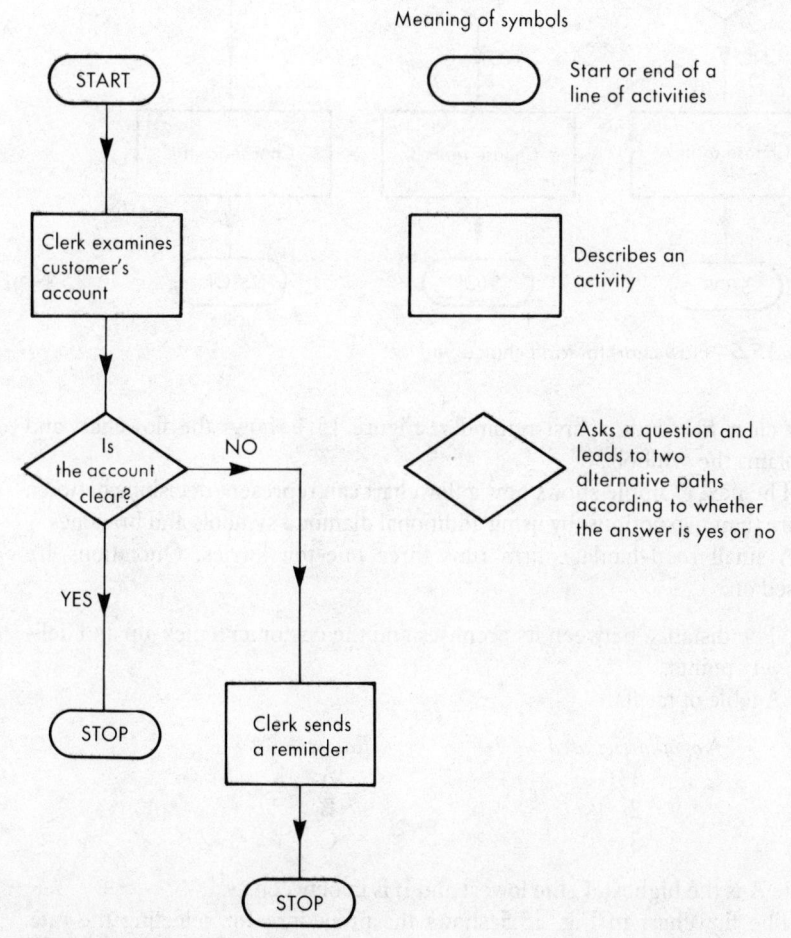

Fig. 15.4 Flow chart of office procedure

and 15.5 are to National Computing Centre standards, but other codes are used.

The foregoing example might be drawn by a systems analyst to describe a simple office procedure in a manual system. A firm's customers are expected to settle their accounts within a month. On the last day of each month, a clerk checks the account. If it is clear, he does nothing more: if it is

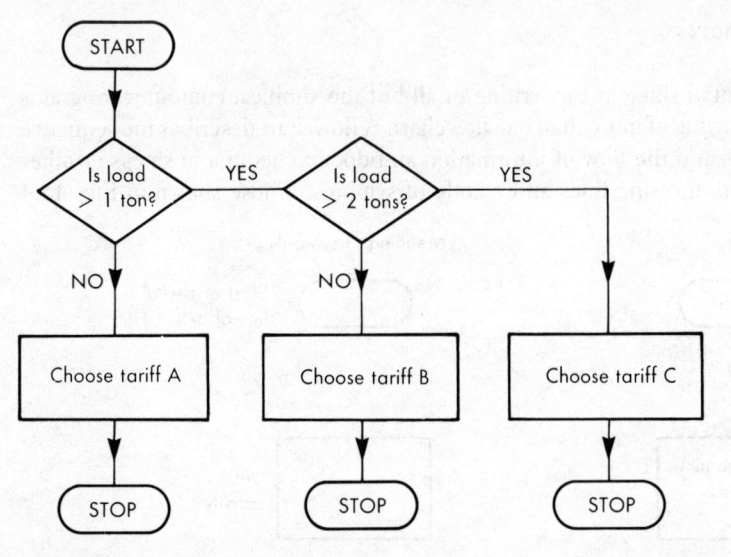

Fig. 15.5 Flow chart for tariff choice

not clear he sends a first reminder. Figure 15.4 shows the flowchart and explains the symbols.

The next example shows how a flowchart can represent decisions between more than two options, by using additional diamond symbols and branches.

A small road-haulage firm runs three one-ton lorries. Quotations are based on:

1 The distance between its premises and the customer's pick-up and delivery points.
2 A table of tariffs.

No. of lorries used	Rate/ton
1	A
2	B
3	C

Rate A is the highest, C the lowest and B is in between.

The flowchart in Fig. 15.5 shows the procedure for selecting the rate. Although this somewhat tortuous analysis hardly does justice to the speed with which a clerk would apply the tariffs, a computer will need to be instructed in this kind of detail if its output is to be correct.

The input/output symbol

This is illustrated by drawing a flowchart for an office process, which is being increasingly converted from a manual to a computerised system, the calculation of the gross pay of an hourly worker with, say, 40 hours per week at standard rate and anything over at overtime rates. The flowchart is shown in Fig. 15.6, where the new symbol is introduced. An example demonstrates how K. Bradley's (works no. 7345) pay for a 46-hour week would be calculated, on the assumption that standard rate is £2.50 per hour and overtime rate is £3.25 per hour.

The new symbol would not necessarily be used in a flowchart which simply described an existing manual system and a rectangle, representing an activity, could be used instead. No confusion is caused by the merging of two vertical lines before the last rectangle because the separate paths are mutually exclusive: the worker has either not earned overtime (left path) or he has (right path). In practice, the stop would occur later, as the calculations of Gross pay would be the starting point of Net pay, tax and other deductions being made. In addition, the final programs in a computerised system could use gross pay in a verification test, because

$$\begin{bmatrix} \text{Total of} \\ \text{all workers'} \\ \text{gross pay} \end{bmatrix} - \begin{bmatrix} \text{Total of} \\ \text{all} \\ \text{deductions} \end{bmatrix} \text{ should equal } \begin{bmatrix} \text{Total of} \\ \text{all workers'} \\ \text{net pay} \end{bmatrix}$$

Systems flowcharts

Although a competent programmer could write programs from Figs 15.4, 15.5 and 15.6 without drawing further charts, the addition of more symbols would enable a more detailed account of the proposed processes to be shown, and the final work of writing the program would be made easier. A chart in this new form would be called a *systems flowchart*. Important additional symbols are shown in Fig. 15.7 and used in Fig. 15.8. Other shapes and line forms are used and symbols, but those in Figs 15.4, 15.6 and 15.7 are the most important.

Figure 15.8 shows a systems flowchart using some of these symbols. A new retail firm is formed by the amalgamation of three other firms, A, B and C, which have recorded information about their customers on separate sets of punched cards. These customer records are merged, arranged into alphabetical order and checked, one customer at a time, on visual display

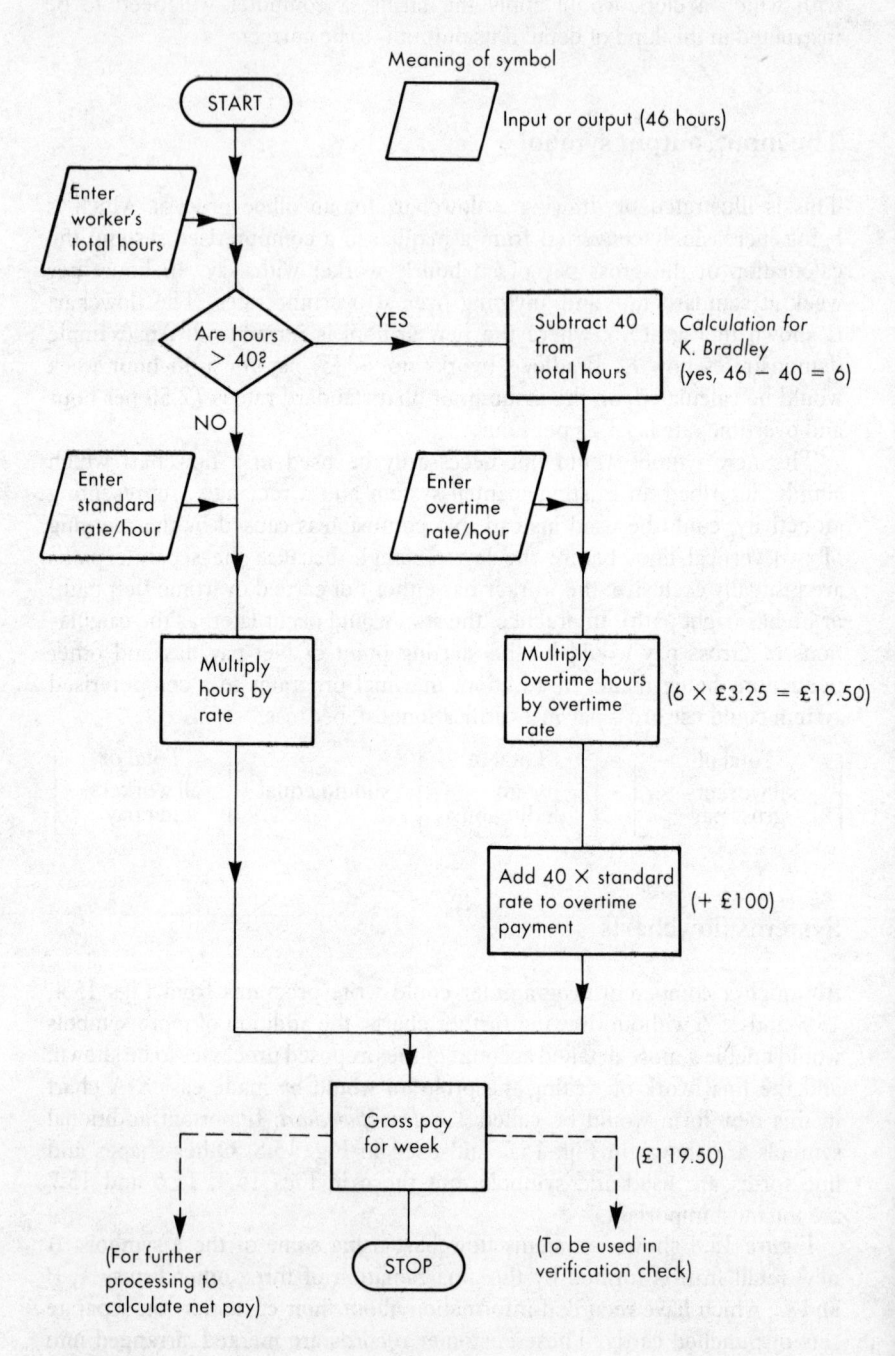

158 Information Processing for Business Studies

Meaning of symbol

▱ Input or output (46 hours)

START
↓
Enter worker's total hours
↓
Are hours > 40? —YES→ Subtract 40 from total hours — *Calculation for K. Bradley* (yes, 46 − 40 = 6)
↓ NO
Enter standard rate/hour   Enter overtime rate/hour
↓   ↓
Multiply hours by rate   Multiply overtime hours by overtime rate (6 × £3.25 = £19.50)
                                 ↓
                                Add 40 × standard rate to overtime payment (+ £100)
↓   ↓
Gross pay for week (£119.50)
↓
STOP

(For further processing to calculate net pay)

(To be used in verification check)

Fig. 15.6 Flow chart for calculating gross pay

against an independently typed list, any errors being corrected by the microcomputer which operates the visual display. Correct records are stored on a magnetic disk and, at the same time, input into a separate program for credit status determination.

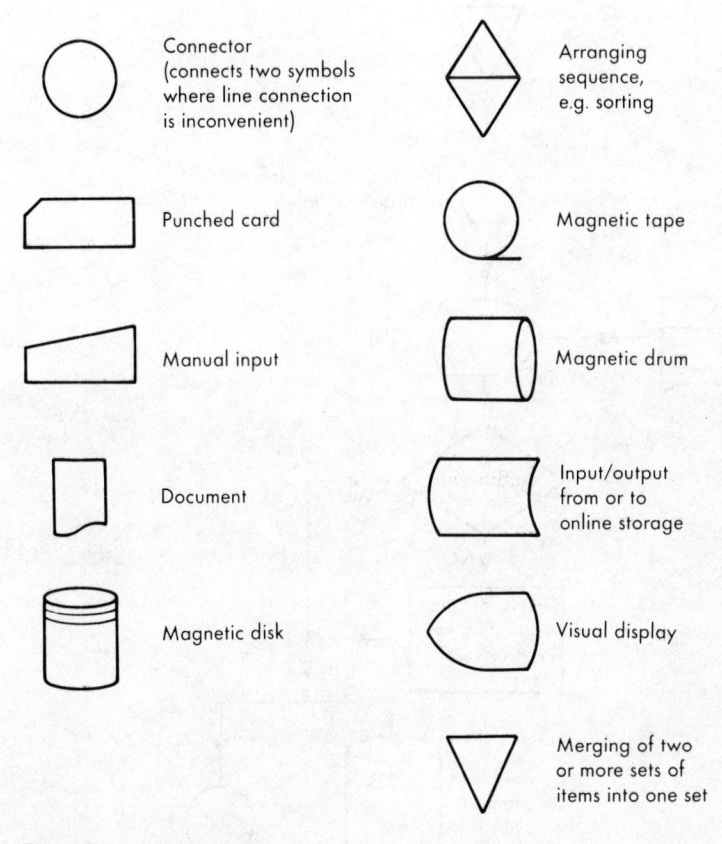

○	Connector (connects two symbols where line connection is inconvenient)
◇	Arranging sequence, e.g. sorting
Punched card symbol	Punched card
○	Magnetic tape
Manual input symbol	Manual input
Cylinder	Magnetic drum
Document symbol	Document
Input/output shape	Input/output from or to online storage
Magnetic disk symbol	Magnetic disk
Visual display shape	Visual display
▽	Merging of two or more sets of items into one set

Fig. 15.7 Additional symbols

Sometimes users of flowcharts systematically add detailed information to the symbols. The new firm codes its documents with X/.../... so that the independently prepared typed list of customers is X/ABC/2, as shown on the document symbol. Y starts the code for documents from the original firms, so that Y/A/1 appears on the punched card for each A customer. A slightly more complicated symbol could have been used to show that each card input was from a deck.

Flowcharts mentioned so far would have led to the construction of application programs. They are also used to construct programs of a more general nature relating to the performance of the computer, e.g. audit programs.

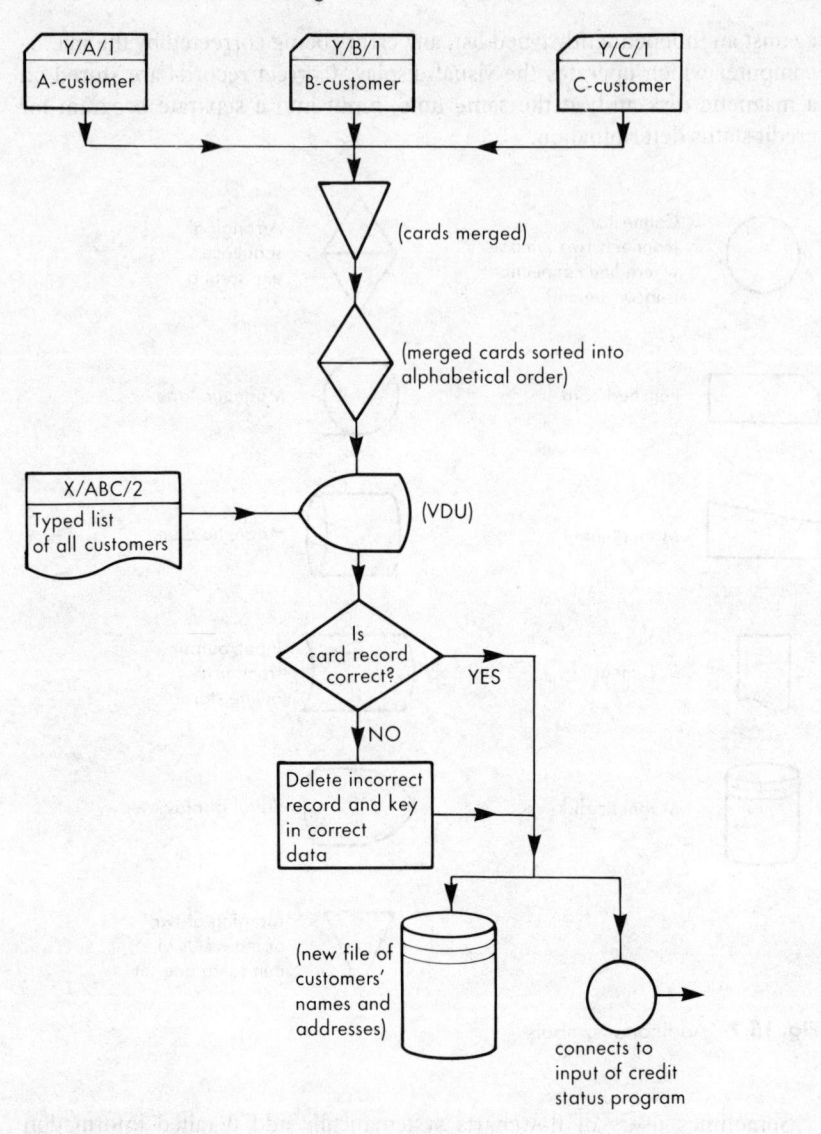

160 Information Processing for Business Studies

Fig. 15.8 Customer record flow chart

Writing programs in a high-level language

Such languages, as explained earlier in Chapter 10, are widely used by businessmen and others who wish to write simple business programs for microcomputers and for whom intensive training in programming is neither possible nor needed. The most popular language today is BASIC, short

Charts, diagrams and software for simple projects

for Beginners All-purpose Symbolic Instruction Code. It was developed in America for the purpose which it mainly serves at present. A full account of its various modern versions, and of all the techniques which are possible with it, would occupy a very large book. This section of this chapter, therefore, will mention important principles and demonstrate some simple applications, so that the reader is not forced to take too wide a leap from processes which prepare for programming to those which follow it. Many readers, such as BTEC students, will already have gained experience in writing and running simple programs in BASIC.

Construction of a program in BASIC

A BASIC program is written in a series of consecutive lines, each starting with a number and each giving a *command*, which tells the computer to do something. The numbers increase as the program continues. A common sequence is 10, 20, 30, ..., etc., which allows the author to add intermediate lines to a completed program, without renumbering the lines which follow. For example, if numbers ran from 10, 20, ... to 140, and a new line had to be inserted between 30 and 40, it could be numbered 31, and the computer would insert it without disturbing the remaining lines.

The following program for calculating the cost of stamps for given numbers of first- and second-class inland letters at 18p and 13p each, illustrates some of the points.

```
10  PRINT "STAMP CALCULATIONS"
20  PRINT
30  INPUT F,S
40  LET A=18*F
50  LET B=13*S
60  C=A+B
70  PRINT C " PENCE"
80  END
```

An example of command in the above program is 10 PRINT, which instructs the computer to print the contents of the double quotation marks, i.e. STAMP CALCULATIONS. The instruction PRINT standing alone gives a blank line on the printout. In this program, the computer would stop when it reached the end of its instructions, i.e. at line 60. Strictly speaking, line 80, which would stop it anyway, is unnecessary, but some programs return from the lowest line to a point above, and stop at a higher line. The END instruction is then essential if the computer is not to continue indefinitely. LET is an *assignment statement*, which identifies whatever is to the right of the '=' sign. In a larger program, a reference to A would produce the quantity obtained by multiplying F by 18. The user of this program would know that F was the number of first-class letters. Alternatively, he could be reminded of the procedure by an instruction which read

PRINT "KEY IN THE NUMBER OF FIRST-CLASS LETTERS AND THEN THE NUMBER OF SECOND-CLASS LETTERS"

Suppose that there were three first-class and five second-class. The keyboard operation would be

3,5

Without the comma, the computer would assume that the number of first-class was 35, and not 3. In line 30, the comma between F and S ensures that the computer processes 3 and 5 separately.

The multiplication instruction is *, so that numerically A = 54, B = 65, and output ends with

119 PENCE

being displayed and/or printed out. An improvement would be to extend line 70 to give a more informative statement, such as

TOTAL COST OF STAMPS 119 PENCE

The + symbol, as illustrated, adds the quantities on both sides of it; the − symbol subtracts the second from the first, and the / symbol (called 'slash') achieves division, e.g. 7/4 gives 1.75.

Calculations such as $3 \times 3 \times 3 \times 3 \times 3$ can either be represented as

3*3*3*3*3

or by the use of the exponentiation symbol ↑. This raises the quantity before it to the power stated afterwards (e.g. in this example to the power 5). In a program, the calculation could occur as

LET V = 3*3*3*3*3

or

LET V = 3 ↑ 5

(because $3 \times 3 \times 3 \times 3 \times 3 = 3^5$).

Editing commands enable alterations to be made without re-writing a program completely. What facilities will be available and how they will be used will depend upon the computer, but on some computers the command

DELETE 40,50

would remove lines 40 and 50 from the above program, and new commands or statements could be inserted.

Conditional statements

A most important facility of a computer, mentioned earlier, is to compare two numbers, state whether they are equal, and if not, which is the greater. Putting it more mathematically, if A and B are numbers input into a computer, then the computer can state which of the following is true:

(*a*) A>B (A is greater than B).
(*b*) A<B (A is less than B).
(*c*) A=B (A equals B).

Most computers can go further in combined inequality and equality calculations, and act on instructions which depend on these conditions:

(*d*) A$\geqslant$B (A is greater than or equal to B).
(*e*) A$\leqslant$B (A is less than or equal to B).

The simplest computer program, such as the stamp calculation example above, runs like a straight north-to-south road with no branches. A program based on the credit status decision illustrated by the block diagram in Fig. 15.3 has two *branches* and the flowchart representing tariff choice given in Fig. 15.5 would lead to three. In each example, to process some values of input the computer would need to leave the main sequence and enter a branch. For example, in the transport program an input of 1.6 tons could be processed only if the computer skipped the tariff A part of the program, and entered the tariff B part. One way is to use the special IF ... THEN ... statement. Suppose a firm had input to a computer a list of men and women, stating the name and age of each person. A new printed list was required with W for worker being printed after each entry of age less than 65 years, and P for pensioner after all the others. The core of the program would be:

```
10 LET A=NAME
20 LET B=AGE
30 READ A,B
40 IF B<65 THEN 70
50 PRINT A "P"
60 END
70 PRINT A "W"
```

If the test does not initiate the jump, i.e. if THEN does not apply, the computer follows the line immediately afterwards and continues until it is told to stop or stops because there are no more lines. In this program, lines skipped by the jump are 50 and 60. But for line 60, the computer would print-out the name of a pensioner under both categories.

As it stands, the program would process only one name from a list. To work down a list it would need to instruct the computer to go back to another name. A GOTO instruction would be written immediately after line 50, and another one after line 70, and the computer would return to the beginning of the program. The opening lines of the program would have been altered to provide a stream of data until the list was exhausted. A more elaborate invoice program later in this chapter demonstrates the technique. The paths introduced by the GOTO instructions are *loops* in the program.

Data will continue to be processed in a loop until the computer is instructed to stop; generally, it is not enough for the flow of items to cease. Suppose that a shop's takings are recorded over a period of weeks and that information needed includes the total takings of each of the six-day working weeks during that time. A convenient method, on the assumption that a day's takings are always positive, is to insert a negative value (or *rogue value*, as it is called) for the seventh day. The program tests the sign of every input value. As soon as it is negative, the computer is instructed to print the last running total of takings, and start cumulating the takings again, starting with the next day's. Another technique is to subtract from a running total a suitable fixed amount and test the sign of the difference. When it is just equal to 0, no more items are put in. If the last item changes the difference from negative to positive it is deleted, and the last total before it is accepted.

Suppose an air forwarding agent is consolidating separate packages into consignments of 50 kg, or as near as possible below, the program could subtract 50 kg from the cumulative weights as successive packages were added.

Run no. 1

Package code	A	B	C	D	E
Weight (kg)	7	12	6	21	4
Cumulative wt (kg)	7	19	25	46	50
Cumulative wt − 50 (kg)	−43	−31	−25	−4	0 STOP

Run no. 2

Package code	F	G	H	J	K	L	M
Weight (kg)	6	9	15	3	12	3	6
Cumulative wt (kg)	6	15	30	33	45	48	54
Cumulative wt − 50 (kg)	−44	−35	−20	−17	−5	−2	+4

Two consignments would be made up. After the first run, the consignment would include packages A, B, C, D and E with a total weight of 50 kg. In the second run, M would be excluded, leaving packages F, G, H, J, K and L with a total weight of 48 kg.

Often processing will include counting numbers of items (e.g. numbers of articles sold) as well as total values. An examination body could count the number of scripts from each centre and calculate the average mark for each centre by using the following program.

```
10  LET N=0
20  LET T=0
30  DATA 75,43,61,20,26,-99
40  READ X
50  IF X<0 THEN GOTO 90
60  N=N+1
70  T=T+X
80  GOTO 40
90  PRINT "NUMBER OF SCRIPTS" N
100 LET A=T/N
110 PRINT "AVERAGE MARK FOR THE CENTRE" A
120 END
```

Explanation

The above program with the data as at line 30 calculates the number of scripts and the average mark per script for a centre with results as follows:

Candidate no.	Mark
(1)	75
(2)	43
(3)	61
(4)	20
(5)	26

giving a print-out:

NUMBER OF SCRIPTS   5
AVERAGE MARK   45

Line 10 sets the script-counting device at 0.
Line 20 sets the mark-totalling device at 0.
Line 40 reads the first item of data, 75.
Line 60 increases the count by 1.
Line 70 starts the running total, $0+75=75$.
Line 80 loops back to read the next item, 43, N becomes 2 and $T=75+43=128$.

The process continues until the last item mark has been read. When the rogue value -99 is reached, the IF ... THEN statement takes the program to 90, which prints out the number of scripts. Statement 100 calculates the average by dividing the total marks by the total number of scripts.

Where the total number of items for which data is to be entered is known in advance, e.g. the number of months in a year, a *decremental* counting device can be used to take the sequence out of a loop into the final stages of the program. In this example, 12 would be entered, and each time a month's data was input the value would be reduced by 1, by an instruction of the form $N=N-1$, and the difference tested. When the remainder was 0, looping would cease and the program would enter its final stages.

Invoice example

Techniques already explained and a few additional ones are illustrated in the program (Fig. 15.9) to print an invoice to meet the requirements stated below, and its print-out (Fig. 15.10). The computer used was an IBM Personal Computer XT.

```
10  LET E=15.00
20  LET S=17.50
30  LET U=20.00
40  LET D=25.00
50  I-1
60  DJ=0
70  LPRINT:LPRINT
80  LPRINT"INVOICE NUMBER..."I
90  LPRINT:LPRINT
100 PRINT"Type in the quantities ordered."
110 PRINT"Economy..."
120 INPUT A
130 PRINT"Standard..."
140 INPUT B
150 PRINT"Luxury..."
160 INPUT C
170 PRINT"Super De-Luxe..."
180 INPUT F
190 LET L=A*E
200 LET M=B*S
210 LET N=C*U
220 LET P=F*D
230 LET T=L+M+N+P
240 IF T<100 THEN GOTO 300
250 IF T<300 THEN GOTO 280
260 LET DI=INT(T*.075*100+.5)/100
270 GOTO300
280 LET DI-INT(T*.05*100+0.05)/100
290 GOTO 300
300 IF A=0 THEN GOTO 330
310 PRINT
320 LPRINTA"Economy at £15.00..";TAB(35);L
330 IF B=0 THEN GOTO 360
340 PRINT
350 LPRINTB"Standard at £17.50..";TAB(35);M
360 IF C=0 THEN GOTO 420
370 PRINT
380 LPRINTC"Luxury at £20.00..";TAB(35);N
390 IF F=0 THEN GOTO 420
400 PRINT
410 LPRINTF"Super De-Luxe at £25.00..";TAB(35);P
```

```
420 PRINT
430 LPRINTTAB(35)"......"
440 LPRINT"            Sub-total..";TAB(35);T
450 LPRINTTAB(35)"......"
460 PRINT
470 IF DI=0 THEN GOTO 530
480 LPRINT"Discount......"TAB(35);DI
490 LPRINTTAB(35)"......"
500 PRINT
550 LPRINT"            V.A.T.    ..";TAB(35);VA
560 LPRINTTAB(35)"......"
570 PRINT
580 LPRINT"            TOTAL     ..";TAB(35);T-DI+VA
590 LPRINTTAB(35)"......"
```
Fig. 15.9

```
INVOICE NUMBER... 1

2  Economy at £15.00..              30
1  Standard at £17.50..             17.5
3  Luxury at £20.00..               60
4  Super De-Luxe at £25.00..        100
                                    ......
                    Sub-total..     207.5
                                    ......
Discount.....                       10.37
                                    ......
                    Sub-total..     197.13
                                    ......
                    V.A.T.          29.57
                                    ......
                    TOTAL           226.7
                                    ......
```
Fig. 15.10

Details
A wholesaler sells to a customer different grades of the same product at prices and in quantities as set out:

Grade	Unit price	Quantity
Economy	£15.00	2
Standard	£17.50	1
Luxury	£20.00	3
Super-de-Luxe	£25.00	4

The invoice should show the total cost for each grade, and apply to the total invoice cost quantity discount, $7\frac{1}{2}\%$ for amounts of £300 and more, 5% for amounts of £100 and more. Value Added Tax at 15% should be calculated and the total amount to be paid by the customer should be shown.

Performed manually, the calculations are:

$$
\begin{array}{rl}
\text{(E)} & 2 \times £15.00 = £30.00 \\
\text{(S)} & 1 \times £17.50 = £17.50 \\
\text{(L)} & 3 \times £20.00 = £60.00 \\
\text{(S-de-L)} & 4 \times £25.00 = £100.00 \\
\hline
& £207.50
\end{array}
$$

As the amount lies between £100 and £300 discount is applied at 5% (i.e. ×0.95).

$$
\begin{array}{rl}
& £197.125 \\
\text{Total} + \text{VAT} (\times 1.15) & £226.69375 \\
\text{and, by subtraction, VAT} = & £29.56875
\end{array}
$$

In practice, values would be rounded to:

VAT £29.57
Customer pays £226.69

These figures differ slightly from the print-out figures, the program having rounded at discount calculation and VAT calculation stages, as will be explained.

The program
Much of the program should be understandable from the account given earlier in the chapter. The intention is that the program should be on visual display and the quantities of each grade ordered, A, B, C and F, should be keyed in. An experienced operator would remember when and where to input this data. Line 100 displays a message to guide the inexperienced. Line 60 sets the discount value at 0, until it is calculated. Note that in identifying inputs (Lines 120, 140, 160, 180) care is taken not to use letters which identify other values. Lines 260 and 280 round discounts to the second decimal place and line 540 rounds VAT similarly. Manually, any value is rounded to the nearest nth place by adding to the quantity a number of the form

0.00...05

(with n zeros after the decimal point) and truncating after the nth place.

Charts, diagrams and software for simple projects 169

For example,

    if   36.418 is to be rounded to the second place,
    add <u>0.005</u>
          36.423

<u>Truncating after the 2 gives 36.42.</u>

If 0.7984 is to be rounded to the third place,
add <u>0.0005</u>
     0.7989

<u>Truncating after the 8 gives 0.798.</u>

In the lines quoted, the instruction INT truncates straight away any decimal, so that 53.46, for example, is treated as 53. The addition of 0.5 in the line truncates to the nearest whole number, but division by 100 produces a rounded second-place figure.

Instructions of the kind shown in line 320 (TAB 35) instruct the computer to print a message in a stated place – in this case 35 spaces from the left.

Decision tables

These diagrams are used in business to show the relationships between the conditions governing routine decisions and the actions taken. They help to explore the various combinations of circumstances. They help in planning flowcharts and programs, revealing inadequacies, lack of economy in instructions, and branches caused by theoretical provision for impractical situations.

To illustrate, suppose that a firm receiving an order for an article checks as follows:

1 That it actually sells the article: if not it refuses the order.
2 That the article is in stock: if not it accepts the order, but promises to supply the article in ten days.
3 That the enquirer has an account with the firm, in which case it supplies the article straight away: if not it asks for cash, supplying the article when cash is paid.

The simplest set of conditions is an order for an article which the firm sells and which is in stock. Such an order is executed straight away. These circumstances are summarised in column 1, constituting a guide for the staff, or 'rule'. Table 15.1 sets out the decision table.

Table 15.1

Conditions	1	2	3	4	5	6	7	8
(a) Is article sold by firm?	Y	Y	N	Y	Y	Y	Y	N
(b) Is it in stock?	Y	N	—	Y	Y	N	N	—
(c) Has the enquirer an account with the firm?	Y	Y	Y	N	N	N	N	N
(d) Has cash been paid?	—	—	—	Y	N	Y	N	—
Action								
(e) Reject the order because article is not sold or cash has not been paid			X		X		X	X
(f) Tell the enquirer article will be supplied in 10 days		X				X	X	
(g) Ask for cash before supplying				X	X	X	X	
(h) Execute the order	X	X		X		X		

Y, yes; N, no; —, not applicable; X, action taken.

A program could be written which showed all eight rules, and every theoretical combination of conditions. A shorter program would terminate statements of rules 3 and 8 at condition (a). Information about other conditions is pointless if the firm does not sell the articles in question.

Programming languages

Although this chapter has shown simple programs in BASIC, a large number of languages are available for programming. Not only does the number increase each year, but improved versions of some languages are being written under the parent name, but distinguished by numbers. FORTRAN, which was designed for scientific work, its name being a contraction of Formula Translation, is such an example. COBOL is a language firmly established in the business world.

A language may be used for a purpose for which it was not originally designed, e.g. some pay-roll processing uses FORTRAN. BASIC has had the advantage of painlessly introducing computing to thousands of users, but it has weaknesses. Involved programs tend to be 'spaghetti-like' because they contain large numbers of sprawling branches, where some languages produce programs in more manageable blocks. An even simpler language, LOGO, has been introduced for teaching children.

One aim of business languages is to produce information reports from massive amounts of data, another is to handle files expeditiously, and some languages have been designed to serve these ends. A number of factors determine the design of languages and their applications. Ease of learning is one, and power – the ability to initiate a number of operations in a small space – is another.

In selecting a language, its compatibility with the type of computer in use must be considered. Some languages are designed for specialised equipment, such as microprocessors. The mode of use is another factor. BASIC, for example, lends itself to interactive computing, whereas some languages are best in batch processing and some in real-time processing.

Short questions

1 Study Fig. 15.1 and give examples of messages you would expect to pass:
   (a) from the accountant to the secretary;
   (b) from the managing director to the production manager;
   (c) from the research officer to the marketing manager;
   (d) from the works manager to the production manager.
Your examples should mention at least one document and at least one message in some other form.

2 Draw a block diagram on the lines of Fig. 15.3 showing alternative branches, describing *one* of the following:
   (a) Application by student to enter a full-time course at a college.
   (b) The submission of a car for an MOT test.
   (c) Application by an architect to a planning authority for permission to build a new house.
Suggest for *any* of the above situations a third option.

3 A shop accepts various means of payment for goods bought over the counter by customers. On *one* flowchart show how the shop would act when payment was made in each of the following ways:
   (a) £5.00 note offered for article costing £4.75.
   (b) £3.25 cash offered for an article costing £3.25.
   (c) £17.56 cheque, supported by cheque card, offered for an article costing £17.56.
   (d) Credit card offered for an article costing £102.

4 A firm has computerised accounting. A customer complains that his last statement of account, which covers three invoices and two payments by him by cheque, shows a debit balance, whereas he is in the clear. The firm has a computer program for investigating such complaints.
   (a) What computer files and written records would you expect to be involved?
   (b) You are *not* required to draw up a systems flowchart, but draw symbols which you would expect to find on the flowchart used in writing the program adding brief notes on how each device represented would be used.

5 You need to compare the cost of laying a new rectangular lawn (i) by turfing, (ii) by sowing seed. You are given the following information:

(a) length and breadth of the lawn;
(b) size of a rectangular piece of turf in centimetres;
(c) cost of turves in £ per 100;
(d) cost of one box of grass seed in £;
(e) coverage in square metres of one box of grass seed.

Write a program in BASIC which will state which method is cheaper for any set of sizes and costs.

(*Hint:* Put your own figures in for (a), (b), (c), (d) and (e), set out manual calculations in fair detail, describe them in a flowchart and then write the program.)

6   The firm mentioned on p. 163 has divided its W category into two, as follows:
   Junior worker – JW – age < 21 years;
   Senior worker – SW – age between 21 and 65.
Rewrite the program to classify workers by P, JW and SW.

7   Study the problem on p.169. Explain briefly why the method would be unsuitable for averaging the balance on a run of accounts, some of which were in credit and some in debit. Describe briefly a program to count and average such accounts.

8   In the invoice example which starts on p. 166 the firm includes an additional grade, Used, selling at £7.50. On this invoice, 12 had been sold. Explain briefly how the program and print-out would be affected by the addition. You are not required to show detailed changes.

9   An examination consists of two papers:
   Paper I – Theory
   Paper II – Practical
and is governed by the following regulations.
   (a) Failure in both papers means that a candidate who resits must take both again to pass.
   (b) Failure in one paper and pass in the other is marked as a referral. The candidate need only resit and pass in his failed paper to pass the examination.
   (c) Obtaining 70% in each paper at the first attempt of the examination gains the candidate a distinction.
   Show the various outcomes on a decision table.

Practical work

1   A charitable body owns small flats which it lets. To qualify for a tenancy, an applicant must satisfy the following conditions.
   A person must be either a widow aged 60 or more or a widower aged 65 or more.
   This minimum age is reduced by ten years for applicants who have lived in the town for at least five years.
   Rent is on scale A for people whose only income is a state pension, and on scale B for other people.

(a) Draw a flowchart for the selection of tenants and the fixing of rent.
(b) Write a computer program in BASIC to select tenants and fix rent.
(c) Show the print-out for the following applicants:

(i)
Mrs Mary Brown.
Widow.
Aged 56.
Has lived in the town for seven years.
Rent on scale A.

(ii)
Mr Bert Hunt.
Widower.
Aged 67.
Pensioner, in part-time paid employment.

2 A society is computerising its records. Table 15.2 is an extract from the manually prepared record awaiting transfer.

Table 15.2 Roll as at 31 December 1985

Enrolment number	Name	Age	Date joined society	Status
0347	Mr Harry Apple	36	1939	A
4712	Mr George White	28	1983	M
3692	Mr William Brown	40	1978	M
5201	Miss Pearl Herney	51	1983	F
0036	Miss Emily Mace	65	1943	M
2444	Mr Bill Carey	67	1964	F
1010	Mrs Nancy Brown	57	1971	M
0008	Sir Septimus Bishop	96	1902	F

Status: Associate, Member or Fellow (A, M or F).
Rule: A fellow must be of at least five years' standing.

(a) Study the table carefully. Two lines disclose data which can be seen to be incorrect. Identify each line and explain the errors.
(b) Design a flowchart setting out validation tests which would reject inconsistent data of the kind you have found in (a).
(c) The society has a rule that on reaching the age of 65, members are excused subscription. Draw up a program in BASIC to analyse the roll and report:
(i) members no longer paying subscriptions;
(ii) members who will no longer pay in one year's time.
Assume that the correct ages are available.

Questions relevant to BTEC written examinations

1 (a) A firm has a large number of vacancies to fill, and invites applications. It will invite for interview only those candidates who satisfy the following conditions:
(i) age 21 years or over;

(ii) at least two years' continuous experience of mechanical maintenance work;
(iii) obtaining at least five GCSE passes *or* one GCE 'A'-Level pass.
Candidates satisfying these conditions are invited for interview, but they do not always attend. At interview, some are appointed and some are not.
(a) Draw a flowchart showing the appointment procedures.
(b) Explain what a *loop* is. Suggest a simple extension to the procedures which would introduce a loop into the chart, showing it in dotted line on the chart.

2 Use the examination rules described in short question 9. Ignore the reference to distinction. The pass mark for each paper is 35.
(a) Write a program in BASIC which prints out the candidate's results, given that the mark in each subject is known.
(b) Explain why a decision table might be drawn up if all the outcomes in question 9 were being considered.

Other examination questions

1 Explain what is understood by the following types of program instruction, and give examples of their use in a business system.
(i) Compare.
(ii) Branch.
(iii) Loop.
(IMS – 1985)

2 Describe, with the aid of an example, the form and purpose of a decision table.
What are the advantages and disadvantages of this means of representing a procedure as compared to a flowchart?
(RSA – 1984)

16 PROBLEMS OF SECURITY, PRIVACY AND SOCIAL CHANGE

This chapter
- describes problems of keeping data and information secure;
- outlines computer audit methods, and other security procedures;
- explains the privacy issue;
- describes continental legislation, and the passing of the Data Protection Act, 1984 in the UK;
- shows important social consequences of computer and information technology.

Security

Against the indisputable benefits to businesses, organisations and society brought by the coming of computer technology, there must be set new problems. In the handling of data and information a most acute one is its security during transmission, processing and storage.

What makes the problem a new one is that messages are stored as minute electronic impressions on media or carried great distances as fleeting impulses on crowded links between computers and terminals. In transit, they may pass through the stratosphere or in cables along ocean seabeds, and be largely beyond the control of those in communication.

Information prepared and sent by manual methods has always been subject to the hazards of fire, water, theft and accidental destruction. Electronic methods attract new risks. Data on a magnetic disk can be damaged when carried at high speed by air through the earth's magnetic field. Small amounts of dust or atmospheric moisture can affect data being stored or processed through a breakdown in air-conditioning in the room housing a main-frame computer. Changes of temperature outside a rather narrow band can be similarly damaging.

Human ineptitude sometimes damages security: records are overwritten, power carelessly switched off from volatile media, and both computers and peripherals can be so mishandled that stored records are lost or damaged.

Human turpitude poses a worse threat. Criminals can divert to their own accounts large funds in electronic transmission with less trouble and risk than hijacking a security van would incur. Dishonest computer staff have new opportunities to steal. One way is to put fictitious employees on the pay-roll, and draw the money themselves. A more subtle method is to route unofficially money travelling electronically between two parties into storage for a few minutes, and remove a portion before releasing the rest. The *salami slice* method is still more subtle. Rounding a figure can produce a tiny surplus, which can grow to a sizeable sum when multiplied through a run of several thousand transactions. A simple diversion, and money due to one of the parties goes to the thief. A more direct method of stealing which has been practised is to interfere with a billing process so that a friend receives goods, but no invoice, or one that undercharges. Another method is to order and receive large amounts of goods and to charge them to a fictitious purchaser, the thief having disappeared from the scene of the crime long before it is discovered. Before computers were installed, unauthorised use of the office photocopier was sometimes a problem. Today, computers are sometimes used by unauthorised people, or in unauthorised ways. The new problem is more serious than the old one, for the improper use of resources may be much more costly, and records and equipment may be damaged in the process.

Direct protection

The best security method is to prevent breaches occurring. Buildings housing a main-frame computer and peripherals should be fire-resisting, with a low flooding risk. Any internal water-pipes should be installed to minimise the risk of leakage. A good air-conditioning scheme should be installed, and an alternative power supply should ensure that it and the computer are kept running during mains power failures. A safe should be provided for tapes and documents. A tight issue system should control the issue of tapes, documents and other moveable material. Extra precautions should be taken to make doors and windows safe. In a large organisation, the coming and going of people should be strictly controlled. Written instructions should define responsibilities for the security of files, programs, etc. A double check of the use of the computer can be obtained if it logs its own running and an independent written log is kept. Operators and other staff should sign on and off. The use of serial numbers on documents being processed helps to prevent loss or error when processing is unexpectedly interrupted. The over-writing of magnetic tapes is discouraged by the use of a ring, which must be put on to the tape before writing can occur. The use of check digits and hash totals, described in Chapter 7, will make for security. Another security measure can be applied when a run of documents contains a standard variable, e.g. a current hourly rate of pay. This is put in before the run starts, and each pay calculation is checked against it. Audit is an important means of protecting security, and it is described more fully later in the chapter.

Indirect measures

These do not directly prevent breaches of security, but are designed to reduce the damage if a breach occurs. Where the generation system operates, as described in Chapter 7, it should be comparatively easy to correct or replace a damaged file. The risk of losing data stored on a main-frame computer when it is not in use can be overcome by dumping, i.e. transferring it to a temporary file. *Bypass procedures* can act as alternatives when normal procedure has broken down. A user can have a reserve computer. In a network system, e.g. one connecting branches of a building society with its head office, a failure at the centre or in the transmission link could mean that the branch could operate independently in issuing mortgages or returning invested money to customers up to stated limits and for a prescribed time, recording on file the temporary transactions, and transferring the resulting data when normal relationships resumed. A *fallback system* brings in outside temporary help, as a computer user might have an agreement with a bureau to accept work temporarily in the event of a breakdown or of overloading. The user should, of course, insure against ordinary and consequential loss.

Audit

An audit in its broadest sense is an organised set of procedures carried out by an independent person to discover whether the numerical and other information presented by a system is what it should be, i.e. whether figures and facts correspond with reality. The auditor reports to his client, but he is not responsible for putting matters right if errors or discrepancies are found. *Statutory audits* are those which the law requires to be made of the accounts of public companies, local councils and certain other bodies; others are *private audits*, and they may cover the whole or part of an undertaking's accounts, and may be made for several reasons.

In a manual system, a single transaction is likely to be recorded in some way on at least one document substantial enough to be retained for checking later if required. Computerisation of a system being audited presents special problems. Electronic records on computer files are likely to replace sheaves of documents. The records are less accessible to inspection, are easily destroyed and can only be read visually after further processing, which may involve machines which themselves are subject to scrutiny by the auditor. Processing is likely to involve fewer people than the corresponding manual procedures, so that independent checking of transactions between separated groups of workers is less practicable. Very large transactions, such as the transfer of funds between different computers or between computers and terminals, sometimes occur with little tangible documentary evidence of despatch and receipt being available afterwards. For a thorough check of a computerised system, an auditor not only needs the means to reveal data in electronic form, but considerable technical knowledge of computing. However, some characteristics of a computerised system may make the auditor's work easier. If the system is properly handled, errors are likely to be fewer than with a manual system, and the auditor can place greater reliance upon sampling methods, as the output of a machine is likely to be less variable than that of a group of human beings. As will be seen, computing methods can be used in auditing computing systems.

The auditor's first step is to lay down an *audit trail*. With the aid of charts and input, output and other documents he traces the course which data follows in passing through the system, so that its whole operation comes within his survey. In some situations, he can *audit around the computer*, treating it as a 'black box', and only concerning himself with the trail either side. He needs then little knowledge of computing techniques, but a fair knowledge of data processing. *Auditing through the computer* means that he follows and understands what is happening inside, and this may lead him to the source of error or discrepancy. Analysing the internal workings of a mainframe computer can be a complicated task.

Various techniques are open to the auditor. He can ask for an ITF – *integrated test facility* – which means inserting his data in the middle of a normal run, and supervising the operations. Hence he can be assured that his test occurs under normal working conditions, and little can be done by operators and others to falsify working conditions with a view to preventing discovery of what they wish to be concealed. The method, however, can be rather disruptive of the operational schedule of a busy computer. A second method is for the auditor to bring a test pack, consisting of all the documents and inputs which would be used in normal processing, including some errors deliberately introduced to test the system's reaction. Making such provision for a particular system may be time-consuming and expensive. A third method, *audit packages*, is more popular. This is a group of programs which tests records for completion, balances for correctness, files for content and the internal consistency of the parts making up the operation of the complete system.

So far, audits described have been directed to discovering accidental and deliberate errors. The auditor would not normally be concerned with the fact that data took an unnecessarily long track in its processing or that an operation was duplicated, when a single performance was all that was needed. A *management audit* would report on such matters, because it is concerned with the efficiency of the system, and not merely the accuracy of its output.

Privacy

Concern over the invasion of the individual's privacy by new methods of technology is widespread, and developments in information processing have attracted particularly strong criticism. Most people feel that certain areas of their lives should be kept private, and that where the claims of public benefit override those of individual right, disclosure of personal information should be the minimum, and its use should not go beyond narrowly defined purposes. The law governing the 1981 Census in this country and the administrative practices followed recognised this. For example, unauthorised disclosure of census material was an offence at law, and enumerators did not cover the areas where they lived. More seriously, breakdown in the new technology has produced injustice – as in the case of a computer print-out naming a person, who as a result was charged, convicted and sentenced, wrongly as it turned out, because the computer did not reveal that two people had identical names.

Today, databanks under public and private control hold data relating to millions of people. Some has been obtained under legal duress, where an applicant for a driving licence must make known, under threat of penalty, previous road traffic offences. Some may have been volunteered by the person concerned, but only for a particular purpose, as when an applicant for a life assurance policy answers a question on the proposal form about his health. Similarly, a written application form completed by a person seeking a bank loan will usually reveal information by which the bank can assess his financial standing. People often give significant personal information without realising it. A computerised library system could, in theory, over a period of time automatically keep a record of a borrower's choice of books, from which a profile of the person's moral standards, political opinions and cultural interests could be attempted.

Technical factors have combined to present the threat to privacy. Data is easily extracted from documents, transmitted by fairly accessible public systems over great distances and amassed in large databanks. The development of quantitative techniques has given groups of collected facts for the government and private bodies a significance which is only just being exploited to the full. Concern over telephone tapping was being felt by the public well before computerisation of information processing developed. Now a related, more serious problem has come, that of 'hacking'. This is the practice by which the owner of a computer can through a transmission line improperly read data which is in a store served by the line, by discovering and using, or breaking, the code which should protect the privacy of the data. Many young people have microcomputers and enough knowledge to attempt the invasion, and are probably prompted by no stronger motive than curiosity or the desire to beat the system. But the potential for damage is great. Not only could confidential information be put in the wrong hands, but information stored could be altered without the knowledge of the holder. A person with a good record could be given a criminal one, with troublesome consequences. It is doubtful whether present law is strong enough to deal with some of these practices, as hacking may amount to no more than looking at private information. Changes in the law would appear to be urgently needed.

A number of arguments support the case for much stricter control of stored data where personal information may be concerned. Access to such data by extremist governments or by political movements planning to set up such governments would give them a powerful weapon of political control. Improper revelation of personal information may make blackmail easy. A lesser ill, although a cause for concern, comes from the storage of educational records or employment history. This may be biased, or irrelevant to an individual's application for employment or promotion within employment; but if it is accessible to an employer it could unfairly affect the person's chance of obtaining work or advancement in a career. The knowledge that confidentiality may be at risk is likely to discourage individuals from disclosing to doctors or medical investigators information that it would be to their own advantage and that of medical science to reveal.

Legislation

For these reasons a widespread demand for legislation has arisen, with the objectives of protecting private information and enabling the individual to know what is being held on computer record about him. Such legislation was enacted by Sweden in 1973. In 1974, the USA amended existing law on privacy to strengthen control over databanks operated by government agencies, creating certain new criminal offences on the subject and enlarging the area of civil redress. The Federal German Republic introduced controlling legislation in 1970 and 1974, and the Austrian government passed a Data Protection Act in 1974. The Netherlands government introduced control through detailed instructions contained in regulations dated 1975. French legislation in 1978 empowered citizens to see stored data relating to themselves, and prohibited storing data on religion, politics and certain other subjects.

The UK took some time to produce legislation on the subject, but pressure increased for a commercial reason. The UK was a signatory to the European Convention on Human Rights, Article 8, which gives the individual a right

Problems of security, privacy and social change

to privacy in his personal life, home, family and correspondence. It has also accepted the Council of Europe Convention which protected individual rights in relation to data processing. We have a considerable trade in data transmission with EEC countries, and had we not produced suitable legislation, this would have terminated.

In 1970 the Younger Committee on Privacy was set up, and a White Paper, *Computers and Privacy*, was published, setting out the objectives of legislation:

1 The activities of those holding personal data should be made public.
2 The accuracy and relevance of the personal data should be the responsibility of the holder, and the subject should be able to check it and have it corrected if necessary.
3 The subject should be told the purpose for holding the data, and it should not be used beyond this purpose without the subject's permission.
4 The holder must take proper precautions against privacy being accidentally or deliberately destroyed.
5 Data should be kept only for a declared purpose, and should not be kept beyond the time necessary.
6 Statistics must not be kept in such a way that individuals can be identified.

In 1983, a bill was introduced in Parliament, but criticism that it was not strong enough led to its withdrawal. In 1984 the Data Protection Act was passed. It appears to meet in general the objectives of the White Paper, but time will be needed to see its consequences. The Act covers subjects about whom personal data has been held in the past, or is being held at present, and potential subjects (e.g. persons selected for a market research enquiry). A Registrar has been appointed, and holders of personal data as defined by the Act are required to register with him. A closing date for registration for those at the time holding data was set at 11 May 1986. The number who actually registered was much smaller than anticipated, and it seems probable that the law has already been broken. The Registrar prepares a list of data holders, and subjects have the right to inspect the lists, and to correct any inaccurate information held about them. Readers who tackle the practical exercise no. 2 at the end of this chapter will discover how far-reaching the Act is in the type of holder and the type of information it is expected to cover. One criticism of the Act is that a partial escape from its requirements can be made by transferring particular items of data to written documents. Some feel that the exceptions given to certain government bodies are too sweeping.

Some other consequences of computerisations

One reason for introducing a computer to a business or other organisation is to reduce costs by cutting manpower, and if a society sets full employment as an ideal, then computerisation could be a bad thing. In particular situations, manpower has been drastically reduced. In car factories, much of the assembly-line work is performed by computer-controlled robots. One building society has reduced clerical staff at its head office by creating a new system of filing customers' deeds and other documents, so that instead of having a number of clerks searching for a particular file, carrying it to a desk and carrying it back to its cabinet, a robot acts upon a computer instruction initiated from the clerk's desk, withdraws the file and returns it to storage after it has been used. Although a word processor costs more than a typewriter to install, one machine with a trained operator and a properly organised work-flow can replace several typists.

The argument that computerisation usually creates local unemployment may be difficult to resist, but this must be balanced against broader considerations. New employment is generated, because computers and peripherals must be made, and software written, and fresh manpower is used to create the network of transmission lines. Computing has now entered primary schools, and text-books and teachers of the subject are required up to university level. When computing is introduced into certain industries, such as oil-drilling and exploitation, expansion is quicker and greater than that brought by earlier methods, so in some sectors computerisation can be said to have stimulated industrial activity.

Undoubtedly, when computing replaces earlier methods, the pattern of employment changes. Most of the staff immediately concerned will be retrained. Some will rise to new, better paid and more responsible work. For example, an accountancy assistant after training could be employed in programming. Some staff who had enjoyed some responsibility might have to take employment at lower status, e.g. in data preparation. In a large organisation, the gap between those on highest status and those on the lowest is likely to increase, with a smaller proportion of people in the middle range. More work will be done on machines, routines will be more demanding, and working relationships will be less personal. Firms and organisations are still in great need of trained and experienced professionals for such posts as data managers and senior analysts, and are tempted to outbid one another in salaries and 'perks', so that staff mobility at the top tends to be high.

In the UK today, unemployment is heavy and increasing, the average working week is diminishing, but output of goods and services has not fallen proportionately to the decrease in man-hours. Some parts of the microcomputer industry such as the market for home computers, show signs of saturation, but the change from manual to computer methods continues in most parts of the public and of the private sector. To judge the exact effects of computers upon employment requires a rigorous, far-reaching and probably difficult analysis of a situation which changes bewilderingly year by year.

Problems of security, privacy and social change

Computerisation is revolutionising domestic life. Shorter working hours and the increase in unemployment has created more leisure time. The coming of cable television, video recorders and computer games has broadened the choice of home entertainment. Experiments have started with computer systems which will enable people to select purchases and pay for them at home, and Chapter 12 gave an example of how the home could be part of a decentralised office system. Microchip gadgetry has already entered the home to operate washing machines and run heating systems. Coffee can be made and cooking controlled through computer programs, and computer-regulated DIY tools are now being marketed. Houses may soon become small computer-kingdoms, not to be entered with the traditional metal key, but through the insertion in a door fitting of an electronically coded badge.

Short questions

1 What new problems for data security have been brought by computerisation which were not experienced before?

2 Explain the difference between direct and indirect protection against security risks, illustrating your answer by methods which a computer bureau might employ.

3 What information on each of the following documents would be of interest to an auditor?
   (a) cheque counterfoils;
   (b) workers' time-sheets;
   (c) claims by staff, running cars on the firm's business for mileage allowance.

4 Explain for each document mentioned in question 3 how information on it could be checked from another document or source.

5 An auditor's report on a computerised system states the following facts:
   (a) Batches entered for processing should have contained 100 invoices each, but there was always one short.
   (b) A worker's weekly time sheet showed a gross pay of £509, based on an agreed rate of £3 per hour.
   (c) In a highly sophisticated stock system, the weekly statement of stocks of sugar was:

Item	Number
1 kg bags of granulated sugar	−346

Comment upon each statement, suggesting reasons for any errors or discrepancies, and action the firm might take.

6 Why would many people regard information contained in the following documents as private?
   (a) A doctor's prescription for medicine to be obtained by a patient from a chemist.

(b) A term's report on a schoolboy sent to his parents.
(c) A completed application for a bank personal loan.
(d) An application for a fully comprehensive car insurance policy sent to a company by one of its customers.

7 A small businessman using a microcomputer, a VDU and several floppy disks realises that the Data Protection Act requires him to ensure personal data in his care is kept secure. Write brief notes for his guidance, explaining to him where risks occur and suggesting practical means of avoiding them.

8 A computer has been introduced to a departmental store, and has taken over payroll, invoicing, till and stock issuing work. Explain briefly how the work of various kinds of staff could be affected.

Practical work

1 Study a small business system using a computer or part of a large system, or return to a system which you have already studied. Draw up a brief report for the computer user under the following headings:
   (a) The need for this system to maintain the security and the privacy of the data.
   (b) What is already being done in the system for this purpose.
   (c) Anything extra which, in your opinion, should be done.

2 Obtain from a post-office an official Registration Pack issued for the use of people who may need to register under the Data Protection Act 1984. Using material in it, and any other which you think suitable, write an article for a weekly local newspaper on 'Registration and your computer'. Include references to the following points, with suitable illustrations:
   (a) data subjects;
   (b) data classes;
   (c) sources and disclosures;
   (d) overseas transfers.

Mention the period of registration, the difference between Forms A and Forms B, period of registration, and the question of fee.

Questions relevant to BTEC written examinations

1 (a) Explain what an audit trail is.
   (b) What problems may arise in establishing it and following it?
   (c) Explain methods used by an auditor to overcome the problems of investigating a computerised system.

2 (a) Describe the reasons for public concern which resulted in the passing of the Data Protection Act 1984.
   (b) For what other reasons are people still concerned about the growth of computerisation today?

Other examination questions

1 Describe the techniques which may be used to ensure security of data in an on-line computer system. (CGLI – Data Processing Fundamentals, June 1985)

2 Discuss the dangers inherent in storing personal data in computer systems and outline some principles which should be borne in mind for regulating such systems. (IAM – Advanced Methods and Systems, Winter 1985)

BIBLIOGRAPHY

Reference
The Computer User's Year Book, 1986, Ed. A. Murdoch Publisher, Business Publications 1985.

Data and Information Processing – General
Anderson, R. G., *Data Processing and Management Information Systems*, Macdonald & Evans, 1983.
Hicks, James O. Jr, *Management Information Systems*, West Publishing Co., 1984.
Zorkoczy, Peter, *Information Technology: An Introduction*, Pitman, 1982.

Quantitative background
Palmer, C. F. & Innes, A. E., *Operational Research by Example*, Macmillan, 1980.

Systems
Beishan, J. & Peters, G. (eds), *Systems Behaviour*, The Open University Press, 1972.

Systems Analysis
Clifton, H. D., *Business Data Systems – A Practical Guide to Systems Analysis and Data Processing*, Prentice/Hall International, 2nd edn, 1983.
Daniels, A. & Yeates, D., *Basic Systems Analysis*, Pitman, 1984.
Inman, K. & Swinburn, J., *Introduction to Flow Charting*, Polytech Publishers, 1972.
Millington, D. *Systems Analysis and Design for Computer Applications*, Chichester, 1981.

Costs and benefits
Bull, R. J., *Accounting in Business*, Butterworth, 1980.
Taylor, A. H. & Shearing, H., *Financial and Cost Accounting for Management*, Macdonald & Evans, 1983.

Management, Corporate Planning
Brech, E. F. L., *Organization: The Framework of Management*, Longman, 1980.

Human Factors
Adams, J. M. and Haden, D. H., *Social Effects of Computer Use and Misuse*, John Wiley & Sons, 1976.
Mumford, E. & Banks, O., *The Computer and the Clerk*, Routledge & Kegan Paul, 1967.
Rothman, S. & Mossman, C., *Computers and Society*, Science Research Associates Inc.

Auditing
Woolf, E. H., *Auditing Today*. Prentice-Hall, 1979.
Thomas, A. J. & Doughty, I. J., *Audit of Computer Systems*, NCC, 1981.

Practical work
Teachers and students tackling assignments and the practical exercises may find the following booklets of help. They were written by the present author to guide candidates for Paper 3, Case-study for Oxford Industrial Studies at Advanced Level. Although the scope is wider than data processing and information processing, the advice on methods and presentation should be helpful:
1 Innes, A. E., *Industrial Studies at Advanced Level – The Case Study – Paper 3 – Notes for the Guidance of Students;*
2 Innes, A. E., *Further Notes for the Guidance of Students (1986).*
Free copies are available on application to The Oxford Delegacy of Local Examinations, Ewert Place, Summertown, Oxford OX2 7BZ.

Dictionary
Disney, C., *Information Technology Dictionary*, Pitman, 1986.

INDEX

Abacus 36
Accounting
  electrical 37
  machines 37
  mechanical 36, 37
Acoustic coupler 134
Arithmetic and logic unit 48
Assemblers 106
Assembly language 107
Audit(s) 147
  around the computer 178
  auditor 177
  management 179
  packages 178
  private 177
  statutory 177
  through the computer 178
  trail 178

Backing store 49, 51, 107, 109
Bandwidth 133
Bankers' Automated Clearing System 127
Bar codes 61
BASIC 37, 105, 106, 160, 170, 171
Batch(es) 81
  cover-note 81
  processing 81, 82, 113, 171
  remote processing 100
  size 81
Benefits 103
Binary 39, 41, 42, 48, 105
  coded octal system 42
Bistable 40
Bits 44, 77, 133
Board-line machines 95
Branch(es) 163
British Computer Society (BCS) 11
BTEC National Specification for Information Processing 12
British Telecom 128, 129
  Golden Electronic Mail 126
  Integrated Services Digital Network 137
  message handling service 137
  messaging services 136
  private circuit services 136
Bubble storage 54
Bucket 84
Buffer store 55
Burst -ed, -ing 101, 114
Bypass procedures 177

Byte   44, 47

Cable conduits   133
Cable and Wireless Worldwide Communications Group   137
Calculations   36
Calculator, desk   36
Card(s)
  cash-point   126, 127
  cash-   126, 127
  credit   127
  telephone   127
Character   41
Charged couple   55
Charts   108, 142, 145, 152–71
Check digit(s)   77, 176
Closed user group (CUG)   135, 136
COBOL   170
Collated   101
Command   161
  DELETE   162
  editing   162
Committee   145
Compatibility   96, 148, 171
Compilers   106
Computer(s)   5, 6, 7, 31, 32, 37, 38, 66, 69, 76, 80, 82, 99, 100, 107, 112, 126, 135, 143, 148, 162, 163
  advantages of   37
  analog   95, 96
  appreciation courses   101, 148
  bank-loan purchase   101
  central   32
  central processor, central processing unit (CPU)   24, 93
  contract   102
  digital   95
  essential parts of   43
  home   94
  hybrid   96
  instructions   37
  internal access store   43
  leasing   101
  main-frame   48, 70, 93–7, 102, 107, 113, 114, 128, 144, 175, 177
  main store   51
  operating   101
  outright purchase   101
  personal   94
  principles of   39
  programs   37, 38, 44
  renting   101
  reserve   177
  services   99–103
  standby services   102
  storage capacity   44
  system(s)   142–9, 38
  techniques   39
  unaided purchase   101
  word   44
Computing departments   3
Concentrator   135

Index **191**

Conditions, decision table 169
Console 108
Consortium 102
Cost(s) 103
   -effective 144
   tangible 103
Cylinder 84

Data 1–12, 28, 31, 38, 39, 83, 84, 94, 113, 164
   capture 76
   collection 76
   filing 145
   meaning 2
   personal 181
   processing 5
   processing routines 76–89
   planned redundancy 89
   preparation 113, 182
   Protection Act 1984 181
   reading 48
   redundant 89
   Registrar 181
   retrieval 145
   storage 32, 48–56
   transmission 132–40
   validation 76–7
Databank(s) 88, 89, 179
Databases 88, 89
   management system 89
   manager 89
Datapost 139, 140
   International 139
   Sameday Service 140
Data Protection Act 148
Decimal notation 41
Decision tables 169
Decollating 114
Decremental counting 165
Definitions 11
Department of Industry 137
Department(s) 112–16
   accounting 112
   computer 112, 113
   data processing 112
   data preparation 113
   information processing 112
   programming 113
   systems analysis 114–15
Diagrams 145
Digital 121, 123
Disk(s) 108
   drive 50
   fixed 51, 84
   floppy 51
   magnetic 80, 82, 84, 159, 175
   magnetised 50
   pick-up heads 50
   read/write head 50

Disk(s) (*contd*)
   removable 51
   Winchester 51
Documents 77, 81, 100, 102, 113, 122, 128, 146, 147, 154, 159
   source 76
   turn-around 60
Doping 54
Duplex 133

Erasable alterable programmable read only memory (EAPROM) 95
Effective management communication programme 138
Effectiveness 102
Efficiency 102
Electronic 39
   calendars and diaries 129
   funds transfer at point of sale (EFTPOS) 127
   mail 126, 135
   office 120–9
Environment 29
Erasable programmable read only memory (EPROM) 95
Errors 38, 80, 121, 146, 159, 176

Facsimile transmission 136
Fact(s) 1, 2, 5, 10
Fall-back system 177
Feasibility study, survey 144
Ferrite
   rings 48
   stores 49
Fibre optic
   glass 133
   transmission 133
File(s) 5, 83, 84, 87, 88, 113, 176, 177
   binary search 87, 88
   bubble sort 86
   'father' 85
   generation(s) 85, 86
   'grandfather' 85, 86
   information or reference 84
   librarian 113
   master 84
   merging 87
   movement 85
   pass 86
   searching 87
   'son' 85, 86
   sorting 86
   stock-movement 85
   transaction 85
Filing, sequential 84
Floppy disks 65, 121
Flowchart(s) 155, 156, 159, 163, 169
Font(s) 67, 70
   solid 67
Formatting 122
FORTRAN 170
Front-end processors 94, 135
Funds Transfer Sharing (FTS) 127

Gateway   128
Geo-stationary orbit   135
GOTO   105, 164
Grand Metropolitan   139

Hacking   179
Half-duplex   133
Hardware   105, 113, 114, 115, 143, 148, 149
Hash-totals   81, 176
Helpline service   136

Immediate access store (IAS)   48
Implementation   148, 149
Information processing   1, 123, 127
   system   32
Information system(s)
   distributed   31
   management   31
Input and output   1, 58–73, 147, 168
   output, punched   73
   output, speech   71–2
   purpose   58
   response, audio   72
   synthesis, speech   71
   voice and speech   62
Instruction(s)   105, 106, 169
   INT   169
   multiplication   162
   PRINT   161
   TAB   169
Integrated digital access (IDA)   137
Interactive computing   171
Interface   17
Interpreters   106
Interrogation   67
Interviewing   146
Invoices   13

Jophenson junction   55

Key   84
Keyboard   8, 107, 126
   entry   65
   key-station(s)   65, 113
   key-to-disk   65, 113
   key-to-tape   65, 113
   stand alone devices   65
Keyline   136
Kilobyte   44
Kilostream   136
Kimball tags   61

Label, tape   84
Language(s)   105, 116, 170, 171
   high-level   105, 112, 116
   level(s)   105
   low-level   105, 116
   machine   105

194 Index

Laser
  beam(s) 71, 133
  storage 54
Legislation 180, 181
Light pens 62
Light-emitting diodes (LED) 66
Logging 128, 176
LOGO 170
Loop(s) 164, 165

Magnetic
  cards 59
  cartridges 52
  cassettes 52
  drums 51
  fixed heads 51
  tape 52, 58, 80, 83
Magnetic ink character (MICR) 59, 101, 127
Main store 107, 109
Management 10
  controlling function 8
  co-ordination function 8
  decision making function 9
  functions 7
  leadership function 9
  motivating function 9
  planning function 8
  reports 10
  structure 154
Media (storage) 39, 40, 41
Mediat 135
Megabyte 44
Megastream 136
Memory 55, 94
  read only memory (ROM) 55
Mercury Communications Ltd 129, 137, 139
Microcomputer 66, 95, 113, 135, 143
Microfiche
  computer output on (COM) 70, 71
Microfilm 71
Microprocessor(s) 93, 94, 95, 171
Microsecond 44
Midland Bank 13
Miniaturisation 56
Minicomputers 95, 135, 161
Modem 134
Modulus 77, 78, 107
Multiple access 135
Multiplexer 135
Multiprogramming 82, 95, 107
Multiprocessing 82
Multistream 135
  access points 135

National Computing Centre standards 156
Nanosecond 44
Network control 38, 123

Observing systems 146
Octal 41, 42
On-line 81
Operator(s) 169, 176
Operational research 108
Optical
    fibre cable 137, 139
    mark reading 60
    recognition 60
ORACLE 128
Organisation and Methods (O & M) 145

Package(s) 108, 109
    application 108, 116
    bundled 108
    unbundled 108
Packet(s) 133
    switch stream (PSS) 135
    switching 134
Paper tape 52, 53, 58
Parallel running 148
Pay-roll, computerised 5
Peripherals 24, 82, 99, 103, 148
Phased changeover 148
Pilot running 148
Plastic cards 52
    cartridge holders 52
Plastic strip 127
Point of sale 135
Post Office 129, 139
    Priority Service 126
    Standard Service 126
Prestel 128
PRINT 105
Printer(s) 94, 123
    choice of 69
    daisy-wheel 67
    electrostatic 69
    golf-ball 67
    ink-jet 68
    laser 69, 126
    line 68
    page 70
    serial 67
    solid font 68
    thermal 68
Printing
    dot-matrix 67
    matric 68, 70
Privacy 89, 108, 148, 175
Programmer 114, 115, 116, 156
    chief 116
    junior 116
    senior 116
Programming 113, 115
Program(s) 82, 84, 93, 106, 107, 108, 112, 116, 139, 155, 157, 159, 163, 168, 169, 170, 176
    application 95, 116

Programs (*contd*)
  construction   106
  high-level   160
  object   106
  source   106
  test   149
  testing   142
Project
  leader   116
  team(s)   116
Protocols   136
Punched cards   36, 52, 53, 58, 86, 108, 157
Punching   100

Questionnaires   146
Queueing problems   38

RAM (random access memory)   95
READ   105
Read/write head   84
Real-time   81, 171
Record(s)   83, 84, 89, 159
  serially placed   83
Register   55
Repeater station   7
Report(s)   29
  ad hoc   29
  background   29
  departmental   31
  exception   23, 29
  functional   31
  management   31
  operational   7
  predictive   29
  scheduled   29
Robots   182
ROM (read only memory)   95
Royal Mail Services   139, 140
Rounding   38
Rule(s), decision table   169, 170

Salami slice   176
Satellite(s)   135, 137
  links   139
Security   89, 108, 175, 176
Semi-conductor storage   54
Service agreement   143
Shift(s)   114
Silicon chip(s)   54, 93, 94, 95
Simplex   133
Situation analysis   144
Society for World Interbank Financial Telecommunication (SWIFT)   127
Software   105–9, 112, 114, 115, 122, 143, 149
  houses   100, 103, 109, 112
  operational   107
  utility   108, 148, 152–71
Span of control   145
Speechline   136

Staff 112–16
Statement(s)
  assignment 161
  conditional 162
  IF...THEN 163, 165
Steering committee 149
Symbol(s) 155
  activity 155
  adds 162
  connector 162
  document 59
  exponentiation 162
  magnetic disk 159
  magnetic tape 159
  magnetic drum 159
  merging 159
  punched card 159
  question (diamond) 155, 156
  sorting 159
  start and stop 155
  visual display 159
System(s) 15–24
  analysis, analyst(s) 23, 115, 145, 147, 154, 182
  boundaries 17
  business 16
  cabinet 15
  central heating 19, 22
  class 15
  closed 20
  committee 16, 20
  computing 28, 31
  design 115, 147
  development 143
  distributed 32, 95
  elements 16
  environment 20
  equilibrium 23
  feed-back 21, 23
  flow-chart 157
  heating 15
  implementation 115
  information 28
  interfaces 17
  life cycle 145
  loops 21
  manual 148, 149, 156
  open 20
  overlapping 19
  packing 21, 22
  shared-logic 123
  solar 15
  specification 149
  stimulus 21
  sub-systems 18
  transport 16
Sub-routine 107

Tape(s) 82, 100, 114, 176

Tape(s) (*contd*)
  blocks   83, 84
  recorder(s)   146
  recording(s)   100, 145
  ring   176
Telebanking   137
Teleconferencing   128
Telephone lines   132
Teleprinter   5
Teletext   128, 136
Teletypewriter   128
Telex   123, 128
  network   124
Terminal(s)   81, 93, 94, 96, 107, 135
  small-dish earth   137
Test-run   116
Time-sharing   82
Time-slice   82, 100
Transaction processing   13
Transmission   100, 102, 126, 175
Truncating   38, 169
Turnkey arrangement, system   100
TV programmes   137

Validation   80, 113
Verification   80
Videoconferencing   136
Videotex   128
Viewdata   128
Visual display unit(s) (VDU)   66, 67, 81, 94, 107, 128, 129
Volatile   56, 175

Waveband   135
Wideband private circuit   136
Word length   97
Word processor(s)   97, 121, 122, 123, 182
  communicating   123

Younger Committee on Privacy   181